PRAISE FOR No

"FUNDRAISING BOOK OF THE YEAR!

Clear, powerful, and practical, it's a must-read for anyone who cares about nonprofits."

Sandra Bernard-Bastien, Chief Communications Officer
The Children's Services Council of Broward County

"This work is a "how-to" as well as a "you can do it" book that sets it apart from the other fundraising books I have read. I encourage readers to pause every time Rachel asks a question at the end of each chapter and write down the answers. This brought clarity to my efforts in ways I never dreamt. A must read!"

- Kim O'Brien, Executive Director
Nonprofit Leadership Initiative

"Rachel's down-to-earth, relatable style draws from many years of experience as a fundraising professional. I have had the pleasure of watching her teach nonprofit leaders. Her book is just as engaging, practical and useful. I can't wait to implement the golden nuggets of wisdom she has shared in these pages."

- Louis Medina, Director of Community Impact
Kern Community Foundation

"Aptly titled, this is an excellent book for those who are new to the nonprofit sector. Seasoned professionals will learn too. The reader will definitely find ways to connect with donors beyond just making the ask. Personal, real, and heart-centered. I feel honored to be one of the first humans to read this marvel of a book."

Pamela Grow, Top 50 Most Influential Fundraiser & CEO
Simple Development Systems

"I felt like the author was having a personal conversation with me. She anticipated my questions and offered answers applicable to my organization's situation. I've been implementing all the great ideas and feel confident I can take my organization to the next level. I was sad when I reached the end of the book and hope the author writes another one!"

Courtney Ford Trzcinski, Executive Director
Canine Assisted Therapy

RACHEL RAMJATTAN, CFRE

NO MORE DUCT TAPE FUNDRAISING

the nonprofit leader's guide to becoming an inspirational fundraiser

Copyright © Rachel Ramjattan, 2020

All rights reserved. No part of this book may be reproduced in any form without permission in writing from the author. Reviewers may quote brief passages in reviews.

Published 2020

DISCLAIMER

No part of this publication may be reproduced or transmitted in any form or by any means, mechanical or electronic, including photocopying or recording, or by any information storage and retrieval system, or transmitted by email without permission in writing from the author.

Neither the author nor the publisher assumes any responsibility for errors, omissions, or contrary interpretations of the subject matter herein. Any perceived slight of any individual or organization is purely unintentional.

Brand and product names are trademarks or registered trademarks of their respective owners.

ISBN: 9798645294274
Editing: Erika Parsons
Cover Design: Ryan Schultz

For more information, email rachel@nonprofitplusteam.com

Subscribe and read more fundraising tips at www.nomoreducttapefundraising.com

Dedication

For my wonderful family
and people doing good everywhere.
Thank you for inspiring me to be better every day
and for committing your lives to changing the world.

TABLE OF CONTENTS

Introduction..ix

Chapter One
Why is Fundraising so Hard?...1

Chapter Two
My Story 15

Chapter Three
My Blueprint for Fundraising Like a Champion 27

Chapter Four
Creating a Fundraising Plan...33

Chapter Five
Rethinking Your Fundraising Mindset.....................................57

Chapter Six
What Donors Want but Won't Tell You 65

Chapter Seven
Writing a Compelling Case for Support 73

Chapter Eight
Making the Ask..85

Chapter Nine
Delighting Your Donors 95

Chapter Ten
Getting Your Board on Board 115

Chapter Eleven
Make Fundraising a Central Leadership Priority 125

Chapter Twelve
Obstacles and Opportunities 135

Chapter Thirteen
Where Do You Go from Here? 147

Acknowledgments 151

About The Author 155

Thank You 157

INTRODUCTION

It's not easy being a nonprofit leader. The tough job of finding funding for your nonprofit is more challenging than it has ever been. Dramatic cuts in government funding for nonprofits, shifting priorities from foundations, constantly changing technology, and an increasingly distracted and disconnected community citizenry make it difficult for you to cut through the noise and raise the money and resources you really need.

Nonprofit organizations play vital roles in communities across the nation. I shudder to think what life would be like without you. You are working hard under immense pressure to respond to the challenging social issues of our time. Some days it feels as though we make one step forward and take two steps back. The need for services is growing at a rate that far exceeds your resources. Larger organizations survive because they have more resources to invest in fund development. However, smaller nonprofits – often those working in under-served communities of color – are most vulnerable.

I shudder to think about what would happen if you close your doors or cut programs because you have difficulty raising sufficient funds to meet the needs of the people you serve. What happens if you run out of resources and have to turn people away? It is no wonder you suffer burnout. You and your staff work long hours trying to help as many people as you can. You and your staff have a front row seat to the incredible pain and suffering your neighbors endure. The question is, how can the rest of us help you - our heroes – as you spend your lives in service of others?

Rachel Ramjattan has more than 25 years of experience in the world of philanthropy. She knows firsthand the challenges you face raising money and the human cost of not being able to meet your fundraising goals.

No More Duct Tape Fundraising: A Nonprofit Leader's Guide to Becoming an Inspirational Fundraiser draws on Rachel's deep understanding of the fundraising landscape and helps you address some of these challenges. You'll see how a simple shift in mindset and focusing your efforts can help you become an inspirational fundraiser and champion for your organization.

Rachel provides you with the framework you need to figure out where you are, where you want to go, and to assist you in developing a roadmap for getting there. She helps you to understand that fundraising is a team sport, not solely the responsibility of your development director or executive director. Better yet, she suggests ways to grow your team, train your board, take risks, and put the FUN in fundraising.

A master storyteller, I'm delighted to see Rachel's trademark humor sprinkled throughout *No More Duct Tape Fundraising: A Nonprofit Leader's Guide to Becoming an Inspirational Fundraiser.* Do yourself a favor. Read this book and share it with every nonprofit leader you know. Fundraising doesn't have to be a struggle. You can do it with the help of this much-needed resource.

Sandra Bernard-Bastien

CHAPTER ONE

Why is Fundraising so Hard?

Every day courageous nonprofit leaders just like you work their tails off to change the world in the most profound ways. You feel overwhelmed by the sheer weight of responsibility on your shoulders. There may be days when you feel like giving up. Yet when you think about the people you serve and the impact you are making in your community, you know you have to keep going and you have to get it right. As an executive director or "Chief Everything Officer," it's up to you to raise the funding to keep your doors open but there are so many things to worry about.

How will you achieve your fundraising goals when you have so much competition from other nonprofits doing good work? What happens if you don't raise enough funds? Who will you have to turn away? Will you have sufficient cash flow to pay your bills on time? How can you raise money when you barely have enough staff to keep your programs running and don't have anyone to help you with fundraising? Why is it so hard to find donors? Why don't more people *care* more about their communities? Why can't you find a wealthy donor that can write you a check to provide all the money you need to help people?

No doubt your "worry list" causes you to lose sleep. You are constantly stressed out about your nonprofit's sustainability. Your mind churns like a waterwheel thinking about ways to bring in more money, while worrying about the consequences of failure. And, you have to juggle all these professional responsibilities while caring for your family.

You are not alone. Every nonprofit leader faces these struggles and dreams of the day when they finally have peace of mind, a talented team to help raise the resources they need to keep their programs running, and donors who support their work faithfully.

Fundraising is hard work, but it *is* possible to develop sustainable funding for your mission with a systematic, methodical, and disciplined approach. You may find it difficult to allocate enough time to fundraising and development. The truth is, you have to. Time spent fundraising is the only investment you can make that will generate revenue for your programs.

No Money, No Programs

You may have tried applying for grants and found it difficult to win them if you don't have audited financial statements or three years of operations under your belt. You wish your board would fundraise, but you can't seem to engage them. You worry you'll have to close programs if you can't raise money fast. You are not alone and it's not your fault. There are structural causes within the sector that create funding challenges especially for small to mid-size nonprofits.

Why Traditional Funding Models for Nonprofits Don't Work

If you're like most nonprofit leaders, you rely heavily on one or two sources of income to fund your work. Special event fundraising and grant funding are two of the most popular sources of funding, especially for young organizations.

The Problem with Special Events

I used to work for a large social services agency which hosted a large black-tie gala attended by about 600 guests each year at a gorgeous hotel in Miami. The staff would spend months securing corporate sponsors, in-kind donations for auctions and raffles, and selling tickets. When I assumed responsibility for fundraising, I crunched the numbers and was shocked to learn the return on investment, excluding staff salaries, was less than 20 percent. When staff salaries were included, we were actually losing money as venue and entertainment costs consumed most of the revenue. While donors spent large sums of money purchasing tickets and auction items, very few of them supported our work outside of the gala.

I'd stumbled upon one of the challenges of special event fundraising. While events can generate large sums of revenue, they seldom yield the profit you hope for when you include the cost of wages paid to staff to plan them. Many organizations fail to execute special events in a manner that generates recurring revenue or renewable donations to sustain their work. Special events are effective but only when you leverage them to acquire new donors and build relationships that turn them into loyal supporters.

The Problem with Grants

Grants can also be a lucrative funding source, but they too have their downsides. Grant research and writing can be labor intensive and there's no guarantee you'll be awarded the grant, even though you've invested staff time or contracted with grant writers to submit applications. Governments change, economies decline, and funders shift their funding priorities. Even though you've received funding in the past, you can't count on this funding being available in the future.

Funders are becoming increasingly concerned about the sustainability of their grantees. They want to be catalysts for growth and impact, rather than ATM machines you tap year after year to keep your programs running. Many are putting caps on the number of years you can apply.

The main problem with special events and grant funding as primary sources of revenue for your organization is that they consume vast quantities of human resources, include some level of financial risk, and don't always yield a high return on investment. Economic downturns and changing priorities of public and private funders can wreak havoc on your organization's operations. Funders and donors want to know, if your funding is dependent on a source that dries up, can you survive? If they feel you cannot, they are unlikely to invest their resources in your organization.

You can likely name a few nonprofits that have failed in their infancy or closed programs because they lost a key funding source. You may know many more struggling to fully execute their missions because they cannot raise the dollars needed. As a nonprofit leader, one of the greatest challenges you face is obtaining the financial resources you need in a world where funding seldom keeps up with the needs of your clients. You're not alone!

Why Is Fund Raising So Difficult?

Concerned about the sustainability of nonprofits, The Evelyn and Walter Haas, Jr. Fund and CompassPoint surveyed more than 3,300 executive directors and development directors nationwide to learn about the development challenges nonprofits face. They wanted to understand why the work of fund development is so difficult. Their publication, *Underdeveloped: A National Study of Challenges Facing Nonprofit Fundraising*, revealed, "Many nonprofit organizations are stuck in a vicious cycle that threatens their ability to raise the resources they need to succeed."

Their findings were not surprising to those of us working in the trenches. Nonprofit leaders:

- Struggle to raise money and identify new, sustainable sources of funding
- Have difficulty finding the right people to build and grow their development operations
- Feel fundraising results fall short of what they need to fully fund their missions

A deeper dive into the data revealed that many of us:

- Lack key fundraising skills

- Work with boards of directors whose engagement in fundraising is lacking
- Work for nonprofit organizations lacking basic fundraising systems and plans
- Function in an organizational culture unsupportive of fundraising success
- Question the effectiveness of the organizations' fundraising

In other words, many nonprofit executives and development staff just like you, lack the essential conditions for fund development success: fundraising plans, supporter databases, leadership and development skills, and a shared culture of philanthropy. Not surprisingly, for seven consecutive years and in the most recent 2018 survey, the Nonprofit Finance Fund's State of the Sector report showed:

- Less than 25 percent of nonprofits had more than six months of cash in reserve
- Most had less than three months of operating reserves on hand
- Close to 10 percent had less than thirty days of cash in reserve

There is a serious problem in the nonprofit sector. Financial instability makes it difficult for nonprofits to attract and retain highly qualified staff and sustain the programs they operate. At the same time, funders and donors are looking for indicators of sustainability before they contribute financially.

External Complications

You may be coping with external factors largely beyond your control such as donor preferences for low administrative overhead costs and grant-making practices of funders that require:

- Audited financial statements
- At least three years of operations
- Matching funds
- Geographic and income restrictions
- Exclusion of overhead expenses

How can you keep your overheads low when you need infrastructure to operate? How can you meet funders requirements for an audit when audits costs thousands of dollars you can't afford to pay? And how can you demonstrate sustainability when you don't have renewable revenue to sustain your operations year after year?

The Good News

Thought leaders like Dan Pallotta, author of *Uncharitable: How Restraints on Nonprofits Undermine Their Potential*, are working hard to educate donors about the dangers of rewarding nonprofits for frugal, low overheads rather than impact. Dan travels the world encouraging donors to invest in charities based on their big goals and big accomplishments even if those come with higher overhead expenses. His 2013 TED talk challenging philanthropists and funders to, "Change the way we think about changing the world" is one of the most watched nonprofit videos on YouTube.

Funders are becoming increasingly aware that grantees need them to provide or fund technical assistance and capacity building (infrastructure to help you grow and scale your organization). Organizations like Grantmakers for Effective Organizations (GEO) are educating their members on how to increase their impact by investing in the infrastructure and leadership development of nonprofit organizations and their leaders.

Many forward-thinking foundations – especially community foundations – have shifted their investment strategy to improve the financial sustainability of their grantees. The York Community Foundation, for example, provides capacity building workshops and purchases large blocks of time from fundraising consultants which they make available to grantees. The Community Foundation of Greater Memphis provides capacity building mini-grants to grantees to purchase technology or to empower nonprofits to engage consultants on their own. The Assisi Foundation provides large grants to independent nonprofit capacity building entities like Momentum Nonprofit Partners. Innovative foundations like the Central Carolina Community Foundation, collaborate with industry leaders like Network for Good, to leverage external funding and provide turn-key technical assistance for grantees without increasing their own workloads or overhead expenses.

Funders are also becoming increasingly aware of the financial burdens created by audit requirements and the barriers these requirements create for smaller organizations. The Children's Trust in Miami, for example, awards funding for the audits they require nonprofits to undergo as an approved expense in project budgets.

You Can Raise Enough to Fund Your Mission

You may be feeling overwhelmed by the challenges of funding your nonprofit but if you've come this far, you have within you the vision, passion, and tenacity to put your organization on the path to sustainable funding. Think of one thing you have done successfully simply because you believed you could. Why should fundraising and development be any different?

- Do you believe your organization is doing good work?
- Do you believe people want to be generous and make a difference?
- Do you feel excited when you invite people to partner with you in making an impact or do you dread asking people for money?

What's Holding You Back?

If you are one of the "one-in-five" nonprofit leaders cited in the *Underdeveloped* study that doesn't like soliciting gifts, what's holding you back? Most likely, it's a fear of rejection, or a fear that donors will think you're annoying. Here's the thing...

"You miss 100 percent of the shots you don't take!"
- Wayne Gretsky

The same is true of fundraising. You have to take a shot by making a compelling ask if you're going to have any chance of securing a gift.

What's the Worst That Could Happen?

When a donor declines your request, "No" rarely ever means *no*. More often it means not now, not this particular project, or your cause doesn't align with our current interests. Some of the largest major gifts I've solicited were the result of a donor declining my initial request.

When No Doesn't Really Mean No

Many years ago, I approached a donor with a very compelling ask – funding a breakfast program for school children from very low-income families. I explained the difficulties students had learning when they were hungry, developmental delays linked to malnutrition, and the opportunity to reduce truancy by providing nutritious breakfasts at school. When the donor declined to fund the project, I was shocked. What is more compelling than hungry, malnourished children in a country where there are no public safety nets?

I could have walked away thinking, *what the heck*? Instead, I continued the conversation and learned that the donor had a passion for sporting programs. He'd grown up in a tough neighborhood and because of his participation in sports, he stayed out of trouble, developed leadership skills, and was able to pay more attention in class. He'd gone on to be a very successful businessman. This donor believed there are many kids just like him, for whom sports is the most effective way to connect especially in low-income neighborhoods. His philanthropy reflected this belief. Children didn't need more instruction; they needed more *fun*!

Thinking Outside the Box

After our conversation, I met with the school principal. She had sporting programs in her school improvement plan, but nutrition was a higher priority. I asked, "What if we incorporate a meal into the sporting program?" A few months later, I approached this same donor with a request to fund the sporting program and received an enthusiastic, "Yes!" The donor was thrilled that we'd taken his advice to implement a sports program and he's been funding the entire program for more than a decade. It's one of his favorite philanthropic projects! Every time he writes his check, he relives the happy memories of his youth, and feels good about making a difference in the lives of kids just like him.

Donors get excited when they have the opportunity to make an impact on a cause they love especially when they have no way to do it on their own. Don't be afraid of making the ask. Otherwise you may deny a donor the pure delight of connecting with a cause they are passionate about and reliving meaningful moments of their lives.

You Can Succeed at Fundraising

The key to successful fundraising is believing you are making an impact on an important cause, finding other people who care just like you do, and affording them the opportunity to enter a mutually beneficial partnership. For every nonprofit seeking funding, there is a corporation seeking to connect with potential customers, a donor who desires to support a cause they are passionate about, or a funder on the lookout for impactful changemakers working to address a social issue they want to solve. If you don't make the offer, you're denying these supporters the solution to a problem they are working hard to figure out.

I wrote this book to show you how to get more of what you want – reliable funding to fully fund and sustain your mission through times of economic uncertainty and change – by creating mutually beneficial partnerships that are irresistible.

CHAPTER TWO

My Story

"The people who are crazy enough to think they can change the world are the ones who usually do."
- Steve Jobs

You may think you don't know how to fundraise, and you may feel frustrated by the lack of help especially if you have a board that doesn't like to fundraise. You may even have moments when you wish you could just hire a consultant with a long list of wealthy donors. Wouldn't fundraising be easy then? The truth is, all good fundraisers started out exactly where you are today. They, too, felt frustrated and had to hold on to their belief in themselves and the value of their work to get through those tough days. In the words of Frank Sinatra, "Work like a soul inspired until the battle of the day is won. You may be sick and tired, but you be a man, my son. Will you remember the famous men who have to fall to rise again? So, take a deep breath, pick yourself up, start all over again."

My Journey

My long, winding road to the fundraising and development profession began in my childhood. I was born and raised in Jamaica, in a mixed-income neighborhood on the outskirts of Kingston. I witnessed the injustice and trauma of poverty up close. "The poor" were my friends and neighbors. Their parents were just like mine; good, hard-working people with dreams and aspirations for their children.

A Life of Privilege

The difference in our circumstances came down to privilege. While my parents were not wealthy, they were educated, small business owners. They could afford to send us to a private elementary school instead of sending us to the local primary school which was severely under-resourced and overcrowded. They could afford to take us on holidays and educational trips to build background knowledge required for learning. My parents could afford to purchase groceries in bulk to take advantage of the cost savings of buying wholesale. The parents of my peers lived paycheck to paycheck and had to shop at the corner store where goods were far more expensive, and paychecks didn't stretch as far. My mother's choice to be a homemaker while we were young meant she could help with homework unlike the mothers of my peers who had to work long hours outside the home, then commute home via slow and unreliable public transportation.

Life Is Not Fair

From an early age, I was conscious of and disturbed by the lack of fairness caused by economic and racial inequity. It wasn't fair that my friends didn't have the same opportunities I did. It wasn't fair that their parents worked really long hours and couldn't afford a car in a country with poor public transportation. It wasn't fair that their parents weren't educated and so couldn't help them excel academically.

I later discovered there were structural injustices in our economy and governance that created these social challenges. While I did not have the power to fix the root causes of the injustice, I surely had the power to empathize with the suffering and work to alleviate their problems. What life experiences ignited a passion for your favorite cause?

Creating a Culture of Philanthropy at Home

My parents were very involved in philanthropic endeavors and instilled in us a sense of personal responsibility for improving the quality of life for others. If I had a penny for every time my parents said, "To whom much is given, much is expected," I'd be a millionaire by now!

As young children, we spent time with adjudicated youth participating in a prison-diversion program. We played with orphans living in the local SOS Children's Village which my father helped co-found. We spent countless hours in the homes of our neighbors, many of whom lived in very humble houses made of wood, zinc sheeting, and dirt floors. In high school,

I visited very low-income, elderly residents living in publicly funded nursing homes housed in buildings that had been condemned.

These experiences shaped my world view. I learned to have fun with and work alongside people from all walks of life and value the gifts they brought to the table. They fueled my passion for community service. We all learned we could achieve more by working together than we could on our own.

Falling in Love with Fundraising

My journey into fundraising began with the help of the Local Lion's Club. Every year, they raffled a Mercedes Benz to raise money for surgeries to prevent blindness and purchase eyeglasses for people who could not afford them. On Saturdays, Dad and his fellow Lions would hitch a trailer with the shiny, new Mercedes Benz to his pickup truck, gather as many teenagers as they could, and head to the local shopping center. We'd spend the day with donation cans in one hand and raffle tickets in the other encouraging shoppers to donate or buy a raffle ticket. We were a competitive bunch of youngsters. Each one of us wanted the bragging rights for raising the most money that day. I was relentless and frequently emerged as the daily winner!

A Gutsy Move

One Saturday, a beggar decided to position himself outside the department store where I was selling raffle tickets. He put a serious dent in my "business" as passersby dropped money into his cup instead of purchasing tickets or contributing to my donation can. I wasn't impressed but somehow, I managed to keep my mouth shut until the end of the day even as the beggar racked up an impressive number of gifts.

My parents recall coming to get me. As a parting shot to my "competitor," I asked if he'd like to donate to the Lion's Club. Dad could not believe his ears. He was horrified!

"How can you beg a beggar?" he whispered rather loudly.

"Easily," I replied. "We are all called to help others and he needs to feel good about doing something for someone else!"

Dad was speechless. I'd taken my parents' teachings to heart and made a gutsy move even though the chances of scoring a gift were low. If you don't ask, you can be 100 percent certain you won't receive. Can you imagine my utter delight when the beggar dropped a few coins in my donation can after my father rebuked me for being insensitive?

An Unexpected Gift

The beggar gave me a gift far beyond the value of the coins he contributed that day or the satisfaction of proving my father wrong. He taught me a lesson which would shape my future career. Since then, I've never been afraid to ask for money to help others. Both the beggar and I felt good when he said, "Yes." This experience helped me to make the mental shift from "begging" to "philanthropy" though I didn't realize it at the time.

I learned none of us has so little that we can't help others. It's often a question of whether or not we are invited. Have you ever made a gutsy fundraising move or taken a risk when the probability for success was low? What lessons did you learn from being gutsy with your asks?

Organizing My First Special Event

As I grew older, my fundraising efforts matured too. In high school, I joined a group that visited the Golden Age Home spending time listening to old timers' stories, combing people's hair and participating in impromptu sing-a-longs to lift their spirits. We observed many senior citizens suffering pain because of dental problems. Being the Nosy Parker I am, I started asking questions. Why didn't these senior citizens have access to dental care? What were the administrators of the home doing about it? I discovered the government-operated home did not have funding to provide proper care and indigent residents could not afford to pay for it. When I spoke with the executive director, I learned he had several dentists willing to come to the site to provide care and a room they could use to set up a clinic. The problem was they had no dental chairs and didn't have time to raise funds. Now, this was a problem I could solve!

Partying for a Purpose

An entrepreneur at heart, I organized a school dance, or "fete" as they were called in those days. I solicited members of my father's Lion's Club, many of whom were small business owners, to become sponsors. My father's company printed the tickets for free. The manager of the local soft drink distribution company donated cases of sodas. Mom and her friends took care of the food. Things were going swimmingly until we arrived at the event and discovered that I had underestimated the creative and entrepreneurial genius of the Jamaican people. Someone from the community had printed duplicates of our tickets and sold them for his personal gain!

We couldn't tell which patrons had purchased the real tickets and which had purchased the counterfeited ones, so we had to let everyone in. I was horrified when we ran out of food but there was nothing I could do. Thankfully the DJ was excellent. Attendees had a blast and we raised enough to buy two dental chairs. Within months, the clinic was operational, and I smiled each time the residents proudly showed off their "toothless tiger" smiles because it meant they were no longer in pain.

The lesson I learned – which is just as true today – is good entertainment covers a multitude of sins! If people enjoy themselves, they won't pay too much attention to the things that don't go right. Have you ever organized an event only to have something go wrong at the last minute? How did you manage the obstacle? What did you learn?

Choosing a Career

When it came time to go to college, I wanted to pursue a career in the nonprofit sector. However, my father quickly nixed the idea saying, "Study something sensible. I'm not going to spend my hard-earned money to pay for you to pursue a career that's going to keep you dependent on some man for the rest of your life."

I earned a degree in Management Information Systems and was recruited right out of college by the Aluminum Company of America (ALCOA). I spent the next seven years in the manufacturing sector as a computer engineer installing computer networks, writing computer programs, and facilitating software training. Though I was proficient and received glowing performance reviews, I wasn't happy. I didn't enjoy the technical desk work. It wasn't what I was born to do!

Looking for a way to give back and for a path to transition to the nonprofit sector, I volunteered fundraising for Missionaries of the Poor. They operated homes for the elderly and disabled all over the world. The work was far from glamorous. Each quarter I'd stuff, seal, and sort for bulk mail 6,000 newsletters, and then manually process the thousands of donations that came in – between full-time mothering two young toddlers and a newborn. I learned the United States Postal Service's regulations regarding direct mail. Who knew one day I'd use these skills to help my future clients?

My Next Gutsy Move

In 2001, in a moment of madness, I volunteered to take on the responsibility for bringing Missionaries of the Poor's reggae musical to Florida to raise funds to build an orphanage in Uganda. The cast of sixty was accompanied by a thirty-piece philharmonic orchestra and I had to host, house, and feed them for four days with no fundraising budget for hotels or catering!

To generate cash flow for the $60,000 in production costs, the event committee and I pre-sold $40,000 worth of advertisements and business sponsorships. Since I hadn't been in the community for long, I spent hours listening to the local Caribbean radio station. I kept a writing pad and pencil tucked into the waist of my jeans. I'd whip it out and write down details about new advertisers as soon as I heard them. This didn't work too well when a new advertiser's commercial aired midway through a diaper change. Somehow, I created a prospect list based on the companies that advertised, researched prospects online, developed a sponsorship package, and drove around with three kids in tow to solicit local businesses. Who could say no to a haggard mother crazy enough to load up three children under the age of five to visit their business? I think some of them said yes just to get me to leave!

Plans Turned Upside Down

Plans progressed beautifully until three weeks before the performances when the awful tragedy of 9/11 occurred. It was a dark time for us all and with the country in mourning, no one felt like doing anything fun like going to a musical.

The event committee considered cancelling the performances, but we had $60,000 of sunk costs and contracts to fulfill. The show had to go on. I contacted a social services agency in New York working with victims and their families. They agreed to accept a portion of the proceeds for the disaster relief effort. People were searching for a way to process the tragedy. A spiritually uplifting musical benefiting victims of the tragedy turned out to be very appealing. We sold 5,000 tickets to performances that weekend and raised enough to build the orphanage in Uganda and help victims of 9/11. I've never been so relieved in my life.

What's the biggest event you've ever organized? Did you have an unexpected set-back that threatened your bottom line? How did you overcome it? How did you feel after the event was all over? What did you learn?

Transitioning to the Nonprofit Sector

With a highly successful, high-profile fundraising event under my belt, I was hired by Catholic Charities of the Archdiocese of Miami where I spent the next decade in a variety of roles: running an elderly visitation program, working as a social justice advocate, fundraising, launching and managing social media channels, teaching, and ultimately back to the world of information technology. I was the consummate *do-it-yourselfer* leading projects to rebrand Catholic Charities of the Archdiocese of Miami, migrate their website to a content management system, implement and later convert a donor database and build an individual giving program to help diversify their funding.

I also co-founded a nonprofit and built a donor base from scratch to support a school of 1,000 children living in a severely impoverished neighborhood in Jamaica plagued by gang violence. Over the last ten years, we've invested more than $1 million in capital projects and extra-curricular programs that have led to extraordinary learning gains for students. The literacy rate and numeracy rates are now 96 percent and 88 percent, respectively, in a school that just ten years ago was one of the most under-performing schools in the country.

I have coached more than 500 nonprofits and helped them to raise more than $25 million of funding for their missions using a simple eight-step process. While I am a Certified Fund Raising Executive, my skills are the outcome of a lifetime of do-it-yourself learning, overcoming obstacles, and being fearless. I was not born with fundraising genius and had no formal education in fundraising. My skills are hard-won lessons of a recovering perfectionist who had to learn, "Done beats perfect, every time!" I hope you'll think of me as your companion on the journey from frustration to hope. If I can do it, you can, too.

CHAPTER THREE

My Blueprint for Fundraising Like a Champion

To become a successful fundraiser, you don't need any superpowers you don't already have within you. At its heart, fundraising is a process of building relationships with people who want to make a difference and empowering them to see the value of collaborating with you to accomplish that. The secret is to personalize your communications so donors see the alignment between what you are both trying to accomplish and then conclude with how your projects will help them reach their goals.

Like most investors, donors want to see results and outcomes that demonstrate they've made a wise investment and are creating a positive impact. How you communicate with donors matters because people give to people through organizations. Your nonprofit is only a conduit. It is important to give donors opportunities to see first-hand the good they are bringing about through their partnership with you and give them the credit for making that good possible. It is even more important to acknowledge their contributions and make them feel like the heroes they are. Without them, nothing you do is possible!

If you want your organization to develop sustainable funding, you must help your stakeholders understand that fundraising is everyone's responsibility; not only the responsibility of the executive director or development director. Your board, staff, and volunteers all have roles to play and your success ultimately depends on how many people you can rally and motivate to help you. You must move fundraising from an ad hoc series of events to a central leadership priority for your organization.

Most nonprofits fail to achieve their full fundraising potential because they operate from the seat of their pants without a formal plan. You know what they say about the importance of planning. *If you fail to plan, plan to fail.*

Fundraising is far more than hosting special events or asking for money. It's a deliberate, coordinated, and continuous process of identifying, cultivating, and stewarding donors so they continue to give and upgrade the size of their contributions. You must place as much value on appreciating your donors as you do on soliciting them. With so many responsibilities competing for your time, it's easy to get caught up in putting out the daily programmatic fires and fail to prioritize donor care.

What relationships have helped you raise funds so far? How do you communicate the impact you're creating to donors? How do you know the content you share with donors is interesting or relevant to them?

In the remaining chapters, we'll explore a simple eight-step process you can use to raise more money.

1. Create a Fundraising Plan
2. Rethink Your Fundraising Mindset
3. What Donors Want but Won't Tell You
4. Create a Compelling Case for Support
5. Make the Ask
6. Delight Your Donors
7. Get Your Board on Board
8. Make Fundraising a Central Leadership Priority

Before you move on to the next chapter, you'll want to gather information about your current funding streams. For each source of income, list the amount raised, and the percentage of your total revenue. Here's a quick example:

Source	Amount Raised	Percentage of Revenue
Special Events	$25,000	63%
Grants	$10,000	25%
Individual Donors	$1,000	2%
Corporations	$4,000	10%
TOTAL	$40,000	100%
# Individuals Giving < $1,000		
# Individuals Giving >$1,000		
# Prospective Donors		
# Board Members		
# Volunteers Not Giving		

CHAPTER FOUR

Creating a Fundraising Plan

You may be feeling a bit overwhelmed by the task of fully funding your programs. You may be wondering how you'll be able to raise money when there are so many other nonprofits competing for funding and many of them work with causes more compelling than yours. Don't you sometimes wish you could raise money for cute puppies and kittens?

In this chapter, you'll learn why you need a fundraising plan and understand the many types of funding available to nonprofits. Then we'll tackle the first step of your blueprint: creating a fundraising plan.

Why You Need a Fundraising Plan

Fundraising plans help you think through and allocate resources (especially time) efficiently and secure the support of all your stakeholders, board, staff, and volunteers. Each person understands their role, and how his or her contribution fits into the bigger picture for your organization. More importantly, fundraising plans provide aircover for saying, "No!" to crazy ideas put forth by well-meaning board members.

For more than a decade, I consulted with a small nonprofit organization that provided homeless prevention services to vulnerable people. We had a well-oiled machine for fundraising with 80 percent of their revenue contributed by individual donors. When the board elected a new chair, she requested a meeting with me immediately to discuss our fundraising efforts. As a professor of marketing at a prominent university, the new board chair was convinced we could do better even though our donor retention rate was 100 percent the previous year and we had broken fundraising records. She proposed three new ideas:

Purchase a huge billboard on I-95 to create "awareness" of our organization. "The problem is people don't know who we are." Her proposal prompted me to ask, tongue-in-cheek, how many gifts she had made as a result of driving past a billboard at seventy-five mph on her way to work.

Send a staff member to every private school every month because these kids come from families with money. They can afford to throw a few dollars in the collection basket. Already short-staffed, I asked, "Who shall we send? And how does this help us build relationships with donors so they will have long-term value to the organization?"

Teach students how to be philanthropic by sending representatives to the local colleges to get kids to give one dollar per month by credit card. She had no idea that the credit card processing fees would consume 35 percent of every dollar, not to mention the cost of sending acknowledgements and tax receipts as it was our policy to send a thank you to every donor regardless of gift size. Besides, college students are barely making ends meet, grappling with crippling amounts of student loans. How on earth could she think this made sense?

This is why you need a fundraising plan! We thanked her for her ideas, explained our plans were already set and prayed she would forget about them next year. Before you can create a fundraising plan, you need to understand the many potential sources of revenue you can tap.

Where's the Money?

Giving USA: The Annual Report on Philanthropy is one of the nonprofit sector's primary publications reporting the sources and uses of charitable giving in the United States. Produced by Giving USA Foundation, and Indiana University Lilly Family School of Philanthropy, the report tallies total giving by fifty-three million households in the United Sates, sixteen million corporations that claim charitable deductions, over a million personal estates, and 82,000 foundations.

The 2018 report is filled with good news for nonprofits. Estimated U.S. charitable giving increased to a whopping $410.02 billion, crossing the $400 billion threshold for the first time. 70 percent of those donations were made by individual donors. The average U.S. household gave $2,271.

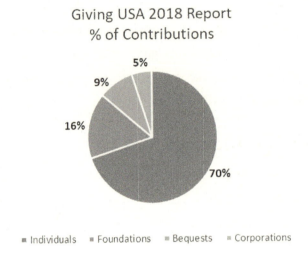

Let's take a look at the four major sources of giving.

- Corporate Giving
- Foundations
- Bequests
- Individual Giving

Corporate Giving

Corporate giving represents 5 percent of all giving, or more than $20 billion each year. As a nonprofit leader seeking to tap into these contributions, there are a few things you need to keep in mind. Corporations' primary motivation for giving is to fulfill their obligation for social responsibility and generate goodwill in the community.

Some corporations give because it helps them to meet legal

obligations. Banks, for example, are required by the Community Reinvestment Act to provide services, economic development, and affordable housing loans targeted to low and moderate-income individuals. They find value in partnerships with nonprofits that serve these individuals.

Corporations tend to support nonprofits whose missions align with their philanthropic values. Lowe's Home Improvement, for example, has a longstanding partnership with Habitat for Humanity; a nonprofit dedicated to building and repairing houses for low-income families.

Corporations seek to grow their customer base by connecting with people who fit their ideal customer profile. Humana, for example, needs to connect with Medicaid-eligible families so they can enroll them in their Medicaid insurance plans. They are often willing to sponsor events like health fairs for people living in low-income communities. Similarly, Northern Trust Corporation seeks to connect with high net-worth individuals. A fundraising event with a high number of wealthy individuals is likely to get their attention.

Many corporations opt to donate in-kind goods or staff expertise before they contribute financially, because they are looking for ways to engage employees. Salesforce, for example, encourages its employees to use seven paid days for volunteering every year. Employees completing all seven days earn a $1,000 grant for the non-profit of their choice.

Many companies want to empower employees to give back, but they lack the time and skills to administer a corporate giving campaign. Nonprofits can leverage this opportunity by providing turnkey solutions for employee giving like branded fundraising pages for a particular service project.

The secret to winning gifts from corporations lies in your approach. You'll raise more money by focusing on how you can help a company achieve its goals than you will if you focus on your needs or the worthiness of your cause. When approaching corporations, describe how a partnership will allow them to leverage your organization's reach, achieve their goals, and promote their contributions to the local community.

Foundation Giving

Foundation giving represents 16 percent of all giving, or more than $26 billion each year. The term "foundation" can be confusing because nonprofit organizations can use the term in their names, even if they are not private foundations. There are many types of foundations, but we'll focus on private and community foundations.

Private foundations obtain their contributions from one or a small handful of sources - an individual, a family, or a corporation. They typically invest their contributions, then distribute the income from the investments by making grants to other nonprofit organizations. They are required by law to pay out at least 5 percent of their assets each year in the form of grants and operating charitable activities.

Most private foundations have a giving focus. The TJX Foundation, for example, likes to support nonprofits that serve women and children because the primary source of income for this foundation comes from TJX Companies which include TJ Max, Marshalls, Home Goods, and Sierra Trading Post. Not surprisingly, these companies sell primarily to women purchasing clothing and home goods for their families. Much like the corporations that fund them, corporate foundations align their giving with the core businesses of their donors.

Community Foundations are dedicated to improving the lives of people in a defined geographic area. They receive funds from individuals, families, and businesses to support local nonprofits. They invest these funds and distribute the earnings to local charities through their grantmaking. Community foundations also offer donor advised funds to philanthropists who want to do good but do not want the work of vetting nonprofits and distributing funds to them. Donors can create donor advised funds, deposit their contributions, and decide what kinds of causes they wish to support. Community Foundation staff vet organizations that fit the donor's giving criteria, award funds to those nonprofits, and report disbursements and impact to the donor. The foundation earns a fee for managing the donor's philanthropy. It is usually a percentage of the funds managed, and these earnings provide the revenue community foundations need to operate.

There are more than 750 community foundations in the United States, and they can be an important resource for nonprofits providing grants, leadership training, and technical assistance. Foundations have varied practices for distributing funds. Most publish funding opportunities in grant cycles with deadlines for submitting applications. Some are invitation-only and do not accept submissions from nonprofits with whom they do not have an established relationship. You can use grant research tools such as the Foundation Directory Online, or Grant Watch to find foundations whose funding priorities align with your cause and geographic location.

Bequests

Bequest giving represents 9 percent of all giving, or more than $36 billion each year. A charitable bequest is a written statement in someone's will which directs that a gift be made to a charity upon their death. The bequest may be for a specific amount of money, a particular item, or for a percentage of the estate. For middle-income households, a charitable bequest will typically be the largest single gift ever made by the donor. Bequests are popular with donors because they allow them access to their funds while they are living and the opportunity to leave a legacy when they are gone.

Bequests can be surprise gifts made by donors you didn't know well. In 2015, Ronald Read, a ninety-two-year old former gas-station attendant who lived a modest life in Vermont surprised even his friends and family with a $6 million bequest to his local library and hospital. Library staff did not know Mr. Read at the library. But for six or seven years before he passed, he quietly spent time there reading and borrowing books. The hospital took care of him near the end of his life and they, too, were clueless about his wealth and gratitude for their services.

More often, bequests are made by donors who have built long and enduring relationships with staff at an organization. In 1993, Ron Magill, goodwill ambassador and communications director of Zoo Miami, befriended an elderly couple that made a generous anonymous gift after Hurricane Andrew. For more than twenty years, Ron visited this couple and treated them like his family. They developed a deep friendship. Over time, their donated annual gifts added up to nearly $800,000. He pleaded with them to let him recognize them publicly. They begged him not to reveal their identities until they'd both passed. They left more than $2 million in bequest gifts to Zoo Miami when they completed their journeys on earth.

You can encourage bequest gifts by inviting donors to leave a legacy through your communications like your newsletters, blog, your website, and when you speak publicly about your organization. You don't need complicated legal jargon to inspire donors. A simple statement like, "Want to protect our children? Consider a gift in your will" is all it takes. Emphasize the psychological and emotional benefits of leaving a legacy, for example, "Your cherished values will live on." You'll want to have a plan in place for cultivating relationships with donors, so they remember your cause in their wills. While bequest giving can generate large gifts, most nonprofits don't receive many gifts of bequests in a single year.

Individual Giving

Individual giving represents 70 percent of all giving, or more than $287 billion each year. Yet many nonprofits do not focus on this revenue source as much as they should perhaps because it takes work to build an engaged base of supporters. Nonprofit leaders may mistakenly believe they'll achieve sustainable funding more quickly through larger blocks of money like foundation grants and corporate giving.

Individual giving is the single most effective method to diversify your income, develop recurring gifts, and improve the financial sustainability of your organization. Think about it. If you have one hundred donors contributing an average of $100 you've got $10,000 of funding. If even ten of those donors walk away, you've still got $9,000 of potentially renewable funding. Compare this to a single grant of $10,000 from a foundation or corporation. If either walks away you've lost $10,000 of funding at once. Individual gifts may be solicited in a variety of ways:

- Direct mail – printed appeal letters sent via U.S. Mail
- Online giving – email and social media appeals made on the Internet
- Special events – in-person or virtual gatherings or fundraisers
- Board giving – financial contributions from your board members
- Major gifts – Large gifts made by an individual donor in one year (typically the top 20 percent of your donors)

Regardless of how they are solicited, to build a strong individual giving program, you need to build relationships with your donors by stewarding them well - thanking them frequently and conveying the impact they are making through their partnerships with you. We'll talk more about this in the chapters that follow.

In addition to the funding sources discussed above, nonprofits have access to other sources of revenue, such as earned revenue. Earned revenue is generated by charging fees for the services you provide or contracting with others to provide services they need.

Fee-for-Service Revenue

Nonprofits can charge fees to help cover the cost of providing services and they can even generate a profit even though that is not the primary objective. Service fees help pay overhead and administrative costs many donors and funders don't want to underwrite. They also help clients see value in the services you provide.

Service fees may be flat costs or may be assessed on a sliding scale usually based on the client's income. Fees are typically lower than prevailing market rates for similar services. Many Catholic Charities agencies provide professional mental health counseling services by licensed clinicians, for example. Some use a sliding scale fee-for-service model charging zero to $50 per session depending on the client's income.

Fee-for-service models are an excellent way to help nonprofits improve their financial sustainability. They also make your organization more attractive to grantmakers and donors. Funders love to see earned revenue because it provides assurance you will be able to sustain the programs they fund after the grant period ends. In the United States, nearly 75 percent of nonprofit income is earned by charging fees for services. The remaining 25 percent comes from fundraising and development.

Government Grants and Contracts

Government grants and contracts can provide large amounts of funding, but they rarely cover all of the costs associated with the contracted program and service such as equipment, site maintenance, utilities, staff, administrative, volunteer management, and other overhead costs. They can be risky as many of these grants and contracts work on a reimbursement basis. Nonprofits must advance funds to provide services and wait to be reimbursed by the government. If you serve fewer people than you project, you do not earn the maximum value of the contract. Yet you've incurred fixed costs unrelated to the number of people you served.

Mandatory reporting requirements can be complex and labor intensive due to oversight and quality assurance standards. It is not uncommon for funding to be disrupted by late, reduced, or canceled payments because a "fine print" item in the contract was not fulfilled. If you're going to use this type of funding, you'll need to have a contract manager and quality assurance manager to ensure records are properly documented and submitted in a timely manner. As you can see, there's plenty of money out there to fund nonprofits if you know how to find it. Now that you know, you're ready for the first step of your blueprint.

Step 1 – Create Your Fundraising Plan
Gather Data on Where Your Funding Comes from Now

Source	Amount Raised	Percentage of Revenue
Corporate Giving		
Foundation Giving		
Bequest Giving		

Source	Amount Raised	Percentage of Revenue
Individual Giving		
Special Events		
Direct Mail and Online Giving		
Board Giving		
Major Gifts		
Earned Revenue		
TOTAL		

It is seldom advisable for nonprofits to receive more than 30 percent of their funding from any one source. While a 30 percent reduction in revenue is survivable with organizational restructuring, a loss of more than 30 percent would make the organization extremely vulnerable. In addition, nonprofits that are considered public charities must pass the IRS' public support test, which requires one-third of their support come from the general public and/or governmental sources. A large grant can easily upset or tip this ratio, causing a nonprofit to lose its public charity status.

What is your biggest source of revenue? What percentage of your income does it represent? Do you receive more than 30 percent of your funding from a single donor, corporation, foundation, or government contract? Are there any potential funding streams with zero income?

Figure out How Much You Need to Raise

Now that you know where your funding is coming from, the next task is to figure out how much you need to raise. Your fundraising goals will be based on your organization's financial statements, your board-approved budget, statement of cash flow, and income statement, etc. By reviewing these documents, you need to determine:

- The amount of cash you have on hand
- What it will cost to run your programs next year
- Spot cash flow challenges or months where you have high expenses without an influx of revenue

What You Can Reasonably Expect to Raise Based on Fundraising History?

Inevitably, there's a gap between your organization's budget and the cash you have on hand to run your programs. Your board will expect you – their Chief Everything Officer - to fundraise to close that gap. And their expectations are quite often unrealistic.

"Just write another grant," you'll hear them say, even though there's no guarantee you'll be funded when you submit your grant application, and even if you are, the process can take months, creating cash flow problems for your organization.

One way to ensure realistic expectations is to create a simple spreadsheet to predict the amount of revenue you can reasonably expect to raise based on your past fundraising history. To do this, you need to review your current funding to identify how much of it is "renewable." For example, if you received a grant from XYZ Foundation, is it a multi-year grant with funding yet to be received, or a one-time grant that cannot be renewed? To measure the renewability of donors, you'll need to know your Donor Retention Rate (DRR).

>DRR = <u># Donors Returning in Year Two</u>
>   # Donors in Year One
>
>Example: <u>40 Donors in Year Two</u>
>   100 in Year One
>
>= 40 percent DRR

Donor retention rates are sometimes different for each type of donor. Your donor retention rate for board members should be 100 percent while retention rates for individual donors may be in the 40 percent to 70 percent range. Corporate donors or sponsors will have their own retention rates. However, all retention rates are calculated using the same formula. You just need to calculate it for each "bucket" of donors and revenue source in your portfolio.

Now, it's time to add two columns to your spreadsheet: your retention rate for each revenue source, and expected revenue. Expected revenue is calculated by multiplying the amount raised last year, by your retention rate. If you raised $100,000 from individuals through direct mail and online giving last year, and you have a 50 percent donor retention rate, your expected revenue would be $100,000 x 50 percent = $50,000.

Source	Amount Raised	Percentage of Revenue	Retention Rate	Expected Revenue
Corporate Giving				
Foundation Giving				
Bequest Giving				
Individual Giving				
Special Events				
Direct Mail and Online Giving				
Board Giving				
Major Gifts				
Earned Revenue				
TOTAL				

Once you've completed this chart, you'll know exactly how much you can reasonably expect to raise based on your fundraising history. And you'll know exactly how big the gap is between what you can reasonably expect to raise and what your budget requires if you are to operate your programs at the level you've proposed.

Closing the Gap

The only way to close the gap between what you need to raise and what you require to run your programs is to raise more money. This is where your fundraising plan can really help you right-size expectations and win the support of stakeholders. As you review your plan with your board, it will be very obvious you have work to do. What will be less obvious is their role in helping you close the gap. You need to ask board members to help you come up with ideas for doing so and you'll "stack the deck" by starting with a request that each of them agree to increase their giving. For each category of revenue, you'll discuss what can be done. Some ideas you might want to consider are:

- Applying for more grants
- Hosting another special event
- Acquiring new donors
- Renewing and upgrading existing donors
- Starting a monthly giving program
- Identifying new corporate partnership prospects
- Cultivating major gift prospects
- Solicit donors more than once per year

As you review each revenue opportunity, write a S.M.A.R.T.

goal for it that specifically states who is responsible for what, and by when.

S – Specific
M – Measurable
A – Attainable
R – Realistic
T – Time-bound

Examples:

- By <date>, <staff or board member responsible> will research five new grant funding prospects with application deadlines within sixty to ninety days and decision dates within 180 days.
- By <date>, <each board member> will develop a list of ten prospective donors who are passionate about <insert your cause> and may be interested in partnering with your organization.

Every board and staff member must have tasks assigned to them, so you have a team of people responsible for fundraising and it is not your responsibility alone.

Next, estimate how much additional new revenue you can generate for each of the S.M.A.R.T. goals identified. Your revenue estimates need to be greater than or equal to the gap between what you can reasonably expect to raise and the amount your budget requires.

Diversify Your Revenue Streams

The key to helping your nonprofit become more financially sustainable is to diversify your revenue streams so you are not too dependent on a single donor or corporate sponsor or foundation grant. Once you've closed the gap, you'll want to assess your plan to see if there are any potential sources of revenue that do not have income associated with them. If so, is there a way to change that?

One area that frequently gets overlooked is the opportunity to generate earned revenue. Many nonprofits mistakenly believe they have to serve people without charging them for their services. There are two disadvantages to this approach.

When you offer free services, you diminish the dignity of your clients and make them feel like "charity cases." Their pride can be a barrier to seeking the help they need. Most of us do not perceive as valuable, things that we receive free.

By providing free services, you are creating a perpetual funding need placing you firmly on the hamster wheel of fundraising. This creates frustration and adds to your stress.

I encourage you to implement a sliding fee scale for your services. This revenue model ensures you provide free services to those that truly cannot afford to pay, while generating revenue from those that can. By doing so, you reduce the gap between the cost of providing services and the amount of money you need to raise.

It is important to remember that your nonprofit status does not mean that you cannot generate a profit on your services. It is simply a designation by the Internal Revenue Service that determines how you will be taxed (if at all) on your business activities. Any surplus revenue you generate can be used to establish a reserve (rainy day fund) or placed in an endowment with a local community foundation so your organization can receive the income on those funds (to help run your programs) while creating a base of capital to generate future income.

Themes and Calendars

The final step of your fundraising plan is to create a theme and calendar for the year so all your fundraising efforts and communications can be cohesive and engaging. Your theme doesn't have to be anything fancy. It can be something as simple as, "Give the gift of *hope!*" The point is, your theme should be reflected in every communication you send, for example, "Thank you for giving the gift of *hope!*"

Sample Communications Calendar with Three Asks

Month	Communication
January	Donor and volunteer thank you and year-end gift summary
February	Donor and volunteer appreciation piece to coincide with Valentine's Day
March	Spring appeal or special event followed by thank you and story
April	Spring is a time for new beginnings success story

May	Mother's Day and Father's Day themed success story/donor appreciation piece
June	Summer appeal
July	Donor story with impact success story
August	Volunteer story with impact success story
September	Client success story
October	Donor thank-a-thon (board members call donors to say thanks)
November	Year-end appeal kicked off on Giving Tuesday
December	Success stories throughout the month with *donate* call to action for donors who have not yet contributed to the year-end appeal.

In this chapter, you've learned that a fundraising plan is essential because it helps you:

- Set realistic expectations
- Engage your board and staff in fundraising
- Prioritize your time and resources
- Say, "No" to crazy ideas proposed by well-meaning board members

You've discovered there are many sources of revenue available to fund your work, including earned revenue, an often overlooked, yet vital source of income. Now that you know how to create a right-sized plan based on past fundraising results, and how to engage board members to increase and diversify your income streams, it's time to turn your attention to your fundraising mindset. In the next chapter, we'll explore the limiting beliefs that reduce our effectiveness as fundraisers and how to adjust our mindset so we can inspire people to give generously.

CHAPTER FIVE

Rethinking Your Fundraising Mindset

How many times have you heard a board member or member of your staff tell you that they don't like asking people for money? Most people are uncomfortable soliciting donations because societal norms tell us money is a taboo subject and they are afraid. As children, we were taught:

- "Don't ask people how much they earn. That's rude."
- "Don't ask how much someone is worth because it's none of your business."
- "Don't ever talk about your finances to others because money fuels quarrels."

The very language we use to talk about our feelings about money and finances has negative undertones that shape the way we think about it and creates limiting beliefs.

- "I hate it when people hit me up for money."
- "I have to save for a rainy day because I worry, I'll run out of money."
- "I need to get a good education if I want to live a decent life."

Of course, there is great truth in these sentiments about money and its power to shape the quality of our lives. However, when the focus is on money itself and our needs, rather than the power of money to bring about good in our lives and the lives of others, we can subconsciously buy into a scarcity mindset and limiting beliefs that diminish our ability to attract donors. The effect of these limiting beliefs is further compounded when we assume others are just like us and subscribe to these same beliefs.

I'm often asked by nonprofit leaders about the challenges of raising money when there seems to be so much competition from other nonprofits also doing good work. This concern about "competition" is an example of a scarcity mindset and limiting belief. As you read in Chapter 3, there is plenty of money available to nonprofits. The problem is most nonprofit leaders and boards do not have the right mindset to fully tap into these resources nor the knowledge and resources to engage donors well. Yet when we try to raise money for our organizations, we fear there's not enough generosity for us to get a fair share.

One of the most frequent complaints I hear from Chief Everything Officers is about board members that don't like to fundraise and refuse to support the organization financially. Board members will often say they don't like asking people for money and they'll make a variety of excuses:

- "I don't like when people hit me up for money."
- "I don't know any wealthy people."
- "None of the people I know are in a position to give."
- "I don't have relationships with any corporations that

could sponsor."
- "I can't afford to give."
- "I already give you my time."

Scarcity mindsets and fear of rejection are the root causes of these objections. People are afraid to part with their money because they worry about running out of money later on. They don't like asking others for money because they mistakenly assume others feel the same way. And they worry that their friends and colleagues will reject or think less of them because they asked for money.

Here's the thing. Every one of us is searching for significance in our lives. We want to feel connected. We want to feel safe. We want to make a difference. We want to feel like we belong to something greater than ourselves. Regardless of income, people are searching for the opportunity to make a positive impact. You may be surprised to learn that people with low incomes donate a far higher percentage of their resources than affluent individuals!

For five years, my family and I took care of a man who was homeless. Mr. Baker, a veteran of the Korean War, lost his beloved wife when his five children were teenagers. Unable to cope with grief and the stress of caring for five grieving children, he turned to alcohol to numb the pain, and became addicted. Eventually, his addiction cost him everything: his job, his home, and his family.

When I met Mr. Baker, he was selling newspapers on the street, sweaty, and filthy, with a bedraggled beard and mischievous eyes. He was a proud man and he would not accept charity. Though he earned very little selling papers, he wanted the dignity of providing for himself.

Every weekday, I drove five miles out of my way to overpay for a newspaper that went straight into the recycling bin just so I could make sure Mr. Baker had enough money to buy a decent meal. Sometimes I'd take him a cup of his favorite Dunkin' Donuts coffee and we'd talk about our families while waiting for the traffic light to change. He had a wonderful sense of humor.

Before every holiday gathering, we would take a huge plate of food and dessert to Mr. Baker to wish him happy Christmas, Valentine's Day, Easter, or Thanksgiving. He got the first serving of every holiday meal we cooked – a reminder to my children that we need to share with others from the "first portion" of our resources, not the leftovers after all our needs have been met. Regardless of how much food we gave Mr. Baker, he would call his homeless friends to share his blessings. I once commented on his generosity and he said, "We all share whatever we have. One day, I might be lucky to receive food or have a good day selling papers. Another day, it will be another guy's turn. We take care of each other and make sure each of us gets a little each day so we can survive."

If Mr. Baker had a scarcity mindset, he would have eaten enough to ease his hunger and saved the rest for later because he didn't know where his next meal would come from. He would worry about other homeless men competing with him to win the attention, and hopefully charity, of passersby. Instead, Mr. Baker was an example of an abundance mindset. Rather than hoard the little that he had, he shared everything immediately, confident that his future needs would be taken care of. Some of the most generous souls are those that have the least.

A scarcity mindset is afraid to ask people to contribute financially to a cause that benefits the community. An abundance mindset says, "I have the opportunity to invite someone to literally change the world. They'll be upset with me if I don't tell them!"

Almost twenty-five years ago, a stockbroker friend suggested we buy shares in an up-and-coming startup called Amazon.com. He was convinced their business model would transform the world. My ex-husband, being a cautious and conservative investor, decided it was not wise to invest. As a young couple, we did not have a lot of money and he felt it was too risky an investment to make. His scarcity mindset led to a decision to play it safe. Decades later, I wonder how our lives might have been different if I had persisted in my belief that we should invest "just a little." Let's just say we could have been millionaires by now. Would I have been upset if my friend had invested and kept the opportunity a secret? Absolutely! Our friend shared his advice with us generously. We made the choice not to follow it. He could have decided ahead of time not to tell us because he knew we were cautious investors, but he didn't prejudge the situation. Instead, he told us about a wonderful opportunity and gave us the freedom to make the best decision for our family. We need to do the same for our donors.

The quickest way to raise more money is to adopt a mindset of abundance rather than scarcity. Instead of worrying about competition from other nonprofits, understand that you are surrounded by unlimited prospective donors actively searching for ways to make a positive impact in their communities. Many of them have no clue how to go about doing it. Donors outsource to nonprofits the work that they cannot or choose not to do themselves. They are searching for projects to invest in and would be highly disappointed if they knew you were changing the world in profound ways and chose not to invite them along for the ride. When you don't offer them the opportunity to contribute, you are denying them the opportunity to meet one of their core needs.

What if you were to adopt an abundance mindset by assuming potential donors want to make a difference and will give generously? Would you feel more confident making the ask? Would it change the way you invite people to partner with you? What if you were to think of solicitations as opportunities to fulfill people's desire to change the world, rather than a process of hitting them up for money? Would you find it easier to reach out?

In this chapter, we learned that the main reason nonprofits struggle to raise money is because they have a mindset of scarcity. And scarcity triggers fear. By shifting our mindset to approach fundraising from a philosophy of abundance, we stop begging people for money and learn to help them change the world. In the process, we attract people who share our passion for the cause we serve and want to work alongside us.

In the next chapter, we'll discuss what donors want but won't tell you. It's not enough to inspire people to give. You have to understand their expectations around giving, recognition, and communication if you want to hold on to them for a long time.

CHAPTER SIX

What Donors Want but Won't Tell You

In the last chapter, we learned the importance of getting into the right mindset before approaching donors. However, this is only half the battle. To be an effective fundraiser, you need to understand your donors' needs and expectations, and your role in their philanthropy, so you can meet those needs. Otherwise, you'll lose them. Often these needs go unstated. You have to take the time to discover them.

Motivations for Giving

The reasons people donate to nonprofit organizations are usually very personal. They may be passionate about a cause, know someone connected to a nonprofit, or love someone who has suffered in the same way as those you serve. As you get to know your donors, you'll develop an understanding of their motivations for giving and the needs they are trying to meet through philanthropy. They may be contributing because they want to:

- Give back or pay it forward

- Feel like they are part of something important
- Live their values and make it possible for others to do the same
- Fulfill a moral or religious obligation
- Leave a legacy
- Feel appreciated

It is your job to discover those needs and show them how they can be met by supporting your nonprofit's mission.

The Importance of Trustworthiness and Honesty

Donors need to know your organization is trustworthy and will generate a positive return on the investments they make. This requires you to be completely transparent in sharing both your successes and failures. You must show them how their gifts have made a difference before you can ask them for more money.

There will be times when things aren't going according to plan. Donors want you to be honest enough to tell them. You may be afraid to share project failures because you worry that you'll look bad, lose money, or anger your donor. However, failing to tell the truth is one of the fastest ways to lose money and donors. You never want a donor to think you're hiding something from them, or they'll be reluctant to trust you with their money.

Several years ago, I led a capital campaign to raise a significant amount of money to build a preschool for 300 children in a very impoverished part of Jamaica. Our team had gone through the painstaking process of getting approval from the Department of Education to build and operate the school, demolishing a derelict building on the property, leveling the site, investing in the development of architectural drawings so we could estimate project costs, and securing commitments from individual and corporate donors to bring the project to fruition.

Suddenly, the prime minister called a snap-election and she lost. The new government rescinded all the approvals previously granted by the Department of Education. You can imagine the disappointment. We dreaded the task of telling our donors the dream we'd been working together to fulfill, had come to a crashing halt. However, we had no other choice. We should have had more faith in our donors. Though they were as disappointed as we were, they encouraged us to think about other ways we could use the land and patiently wait for the right time to move forward. We offered to return the contributions they had made and not a single donor accepted our offer because they trusted us and knew we would be good stewards of their gifts. Recently, that same government requested we partner with them to build a preschool and we are in the midst of another capital campaign to make it happen.

The Importance of Listening

In any good relationship, there needs to be good communication. We need to spend even more time listening than we do talking. There's an old adage in fundraising that says, "If you want money, ask for advice. If you want advice, asked for money."

Donors have wisdom, experience, and talents that can be very helpful in achieving your nonprofit's mission. The more opportunities you give them to share advice and work alongside you, the more invested they'll be in your work. This is why it's essential to create opportunities for your donors to get involved. If a picture is worth a thousand words, a site visit or volunteer experience is worth a million! There's nothing as powerful for a donor as the opportunity to meet firsthand – and possibly serve – someone being helped by their gifts. Studies show that donors who volunteer or attend a special event are more likely to make or increase their financial contributions. This is especially true for millennials who like to donate after volunteering.

Donors are Hardwired for Giving

From an early age, every human being learns the importance of sharing their resources. Parents, educators, leaders of faith, philosophers, and even elected officials encourage us to be charitable. We learn that it is better to give than to receive because it feels good to help someone in need and prevents us from living selfishly.

"For it is in giving that we receive."
- Saint Francis of Assisi

"The sole meaning of life is to serve humanity."
- Leo Tolstoy

*"We make a living by what we get;
we make a life by what we give."*
- Winston Churchill

Lessons on giving may be rooted in morality and good citizenship but scientific research also shows that sharing one's time, talents, and treasure can help someone find purpose in his or her life, endure and overcome difficult situations, and find fulfillment. Our brains are wired for connections with others and a sense of belonging or community. This is why a philosophy of scarcity is completely unhelpful in the world of fundraising. People hard-wired for generosity create an abundance of opportunities for fundraisers. Imagine how much easier it would be to raise money if we honestly believed that people are not only wired to be generous, but they receive something they desire; that sense of connection with others through philanthropy. By paying attention to their desires and affording them the opportunity to make a difference in a way they cannot achieve by themselves, you'll bring them great joy. Who doesn't like bringing joy to others?

Fundraising is the process of connecting someone to his or her purpose in a way that makes them feel good about giving. You are the guide that helps them find fulfillment. To be a good guide, you must understand what your "follower" is seeking. Donors don't need *you* in particular, to be fulfilled in their lives and in their giving. In fact, they will test you to see if you appreciate them and wait to see if you will invest the time to build a mutually rewarding relationship. They expect you to take the time to learn about their passions, values and dreams and communicate with them based on their interests. If you don't treat them like special friends, there are plenty of other organizations where they can direct their gifts. They will find other guides and support those projects instead. Remember people give to people *through* organizations. Your job is to delight your donors in ways that make them feel good about the investments they've made in your organization even if they say they don't want to be acknowledged!

Partnership: Working Together to Change the World

While people are generous, they want to be treated as valued partners deeply connected to your mission and outcomes. This is why it's so important to communicate regularly by sending heartfelt acknowledgements, updates on the impact you are creating together, and invitations for them to come onsite (if possible) to see their gifts at work. In Chapter 9, we'll learn how to create communications that convey confidence that the project or program donors supported will achieve the outcomes you said they would. When you're successful, you'll hear donors say, "I get so much more out of this than I give."

When you fail to treat donors as valued partners, your retention rates will be lower, and you may observe "donor fatigue." Donor fatigue occurs when your relationship with donors is transactional or focused on solicitation rather than building a mutually rewarding partnership with your supporters. In transactional relationships donors feel more like ATM machines than treasured partners because the only time they hear from you is when you're asking for money.

How are donors treated by your organization? What communications do they receive after making a gift? What would your donors say about the way your organization treats them? Are you one of their favorite charities?

In this chapter, you've learned that donors are not altruistic by nature. Like most of us, they give because it feels good, and they want to feel connected to something greater than themselves. Donors have high expectations even if they tell you they don't. They are sick and tired of supporting ungrateful nonprofits and will quickly abandon you if you do not treat them with the respect they deserve.

Now that you understand what mindset you need to be successful, and what makes donors tick, it's time to learn how to create a compelling case for support for your organization. In the next chapter, you'll learn how to tell you organization's story in a way that inspires donors to invest in your mission.

CHAPTER SEVEN

Writing a Compelling Case for Support

To raise money successfully, you need more than the right fundraising mindset and an understanding of what donors want. You must have a funding opportunity that can help a donor accomplish their philanthropic goals while providing funding for your organization. This is called a case for support or case statement.

Your case for support is the single most important internal document you'll create. It compels people to join your board, volunteer, become employees, and most importantly, make financial contributions to your nonprofit. This document will become the basis for brochures, foundation grant proposals, direct mail letters, newsletters, website and social media content, press releases, presentations, and in-person solicitations.

Why You Need a Case for Support

Your case statement helps you establish credibility by presenting a compelling solution to a community problem and positions your organization as the best nonprofit partner to address the issue. It helps supporters understand how they can make an impact by investing in your organization. It helps to ensure messaging consistency because every board member, employee, and volunteer is drawing from the same playbook.

Components of a Case Statement

Usually, case statements include a brief history of your organization, an explanation of the problem you are working to address, an outline of your solution, a description of your unique ability to solve the problem, and clear plans, goals, and measurable outcomes to assess the impact you're working to achieve.

History

Your *brief* history should explain why and how your organization came into existence and include language to explain the social and demographic context and issues that led to the formation of your organization. You want to help the donor understand your incomparable mission, in a way that leads them to conclude that you are trustworthy, have a track record of success, and are the best possible partner for them to work alongside.

Explanation of the Problem

A case for support requires background information to help a potential donor understand the underlying causes and consequences of the social problem that creates the need for your project or program. In creating the case for support for the preschool in Jamaica, we had to explain the government's lack of funding to build schools, the vast number of children who enter primary school without any early childhood education, the learning challenges of children growing up with illiterate parents, and how the prevalence of low-income, single-parent households has led to malnutrition and learning differences in children. We had to explain the urgency of these challenges. If we don't provide children with access to adequate nutrition and quality education, they become vulnerable to human trafficking and other criminal activities.

The social and demographic context helps prospective donors understand situations they likely have never encountered personally in their lives. Without this context, it is difficult for them to imagine that others do not live with the privileges and advantages they may take for granted. Once they understand the social and demographic context, they will use logic, reasoning, and emotion and to decide whether to invest in your project.

Your Solution

Having established your organization's credibility and explained the social and demographic context behind your work or project, it's time to showcase your solution to solving the problem. Your plan for solving the problem needs to show an innovative and collaborative approach and get the donor's attention. No doubt, there will be many organizations working to address this problem. Why should a donor invest in your particular opportunity? How will you save or change lives?

In soliciting funds for the preschool, we explained we'd

be the first preschool in Jamaica to test toddlers and young children for disabilities and incorporate on-site speech, occupational, and physical therapy programs. While this is not a particularly innovative approach in the United States where early identification is automatic, in third world countries, this is rarely the case. Most children with learning disabilities are not identified until they are in first grade because most do not attend preschool and come from poor families unable to test children privately.

Your Unique Role

To win the support of donors, you have to explain why you are uniquely positioned to address the problem. What makes your organization the best qualified to respond to the problem, meet the challenge, and render the proposed service? In other words, you have to differentiate yourself from other nonprofits serving the same population or need.

In our preschool's case for support, we highlighted the fact that we already operated the only primary school in the community and had established relationships with parents. This was important because in this low-income neighborhood, outsiders are perceived as threats and were not welcome in the community. Having lived and served the people for more than a decade, our school principal is trusted, revered, and has a track record of outcomes that make the community proud – having taken the school from being one of the most under-performing schools in the country to one of the highest performing schools on par with affluent institutions attended by the children of the elite.

Plan and Goals

Once you've established your credibility and differentiated yourself from other nonprofits working to address the same problem, it's time to share your specific plans and goals for the project. This portion of your case for support helps donors logically conclude that investing in your project makes sense.

Donors want to understand who is responsible for finding the financing for the proposed plan and what sources of funding you are planning to leverage. Most people are reluctant to finance 100 percent of your project. They want to know others have vetted your ideas and reached the same conclusion they have: that your project is worthy of funding. Your explanation of how the project will be financed helps donors answer their unasked question: how will my contribution make a difference especially if it's a small portion of the total needed to be successful?

Once you've reassured supporters that your financing plan is in place, you'll need to explain how you will measure success. Donors want to see outcomes, not outputs. They aren't so interested in how many meals you served or how many nights shelter you provided. They want to know how you transformed lives. They are less interested in how many hours of remedial education you provided and more interested in the number of children who improved their academic performance by one or more letter grades.

By explaining the goals and metrics you'll use to manage the project, you reassure them that you've planned ahead and have in place the tools you need to monitor progress, thereby increasing the likelihood of generating a positive return on their investment.

Speaking to Different Types of Donors

Each of the case statement components described above, helps you logically justify to a donor why they should invest. However, you still need to "close the deal." Emotions and opportunities for transformation are the key. Your request has to not only make logical sense. It also needs to trigger strong emotions in your donor and speak to the transformations (impact) they can make possible. To do this well, you need to understand there are three different types of donors.

- Rational donors make decisions with their heads. Your case statement has to lead them to conclude that what they are being asked to do makes sense and they understand why it's important.
- Emotional donors decide with their hearts. They need to be able to identify with your mission and programs. This is usually because they know someone that has been affected or impacted directly by your work or cause, so they want to help.
- Transformational donors are seeking to solve big problems and want to leverage their resources to change the world. These donors are sometimes called "halo" donors.

Use language that triggers emotions and feelings while logically outlining the need, plan, and impact you'll create together. Your case for support is as much a compelling story as it is a logical outline and explanation of your credibility and plan. The more you can trigger strong feelings such as anger, empathy, and hope, and speak to the impact donors have the opportunity to make, the more successful you'll be in winning financial support.

Donors want brief, clear, requests that are easy to understand. Don't "beat around the bush" awkwardly. They are busy people who are not interested in wading through long and vague content to figure out what you're asking for. The more concise you can be, the better. Use simple language to show them how they can make a difference even if they can only contribute a small gift. They want to know exactly what it costs to help, how their money will be used, and have choices available so they can decide on the level of support that they wish to provide.

Case for Support Checklist

Below is a short checklist to help you determine whether your case for support is likely to resonate with others.

- Is your case statement emotional and rational?
- Have you explained how each gift will create impact?
- Have you provided proof that your plan will work?
- Is the opportunity clearly outlined with a specific ask?
- Is your plan logical and reasonable?
- Is your case statement readable, and free of jargon or acronyms?

Quick Example

The best way to learn how to write your case for support is to take a look at a few examples. We'll use an excerpt rather than a full case statement for this exercise. "Our organization has set a goal of raising $100,000. Will you consider making a gift of $5,000 in support of this goal?"

This case statement is so vague that it will trigger an endless amount of questions in the minds of prospective donors. Who are you? Why do you need $100,000? Why is this my problem? Why do you need $5,000? Why not $500, or $1,000, or even $10,000? What will the money be used for specifically? How will I know you invested my hard-earned contribution well? What's your plan? How will you measure success? Suppose you were to fill in a few blanks...

"There are 500 homeless, hungry children in Broward County. We need an additional $25,000 to feed them so we've increased our fundraising goal to $100,000. Will you donate $5,000 so we don't have to turn children away?"

While this case statement is much improved and answers the question of why a donor should care – children will go hungry - it still leaves too many unanswered questions for the donor. Who are you? Why do you need $100,000 if it only costs $25,000 to feed these children? How will I know you invested my funds well? What outcomes will you achieve by feeding these children? Let's include a few more details...

"Do you remember long, *fun* days of summer when you were a child? Sadly, 500 children in Broward County will not know this joy. Instead, they'll cope with growling stomachs and throbbing headaches when they lose access to free meals at school. It doesn't have to be this way! For just $25,000, you and I can feed these sweet children while school's out. Like you, for the past thirty years, Help Children Thrive has believed every child deserves carefree summers of fun. Will you make a gift of $5,000 so they can make happy memories this summer?"

This case statement is far more powerful than the first two examples. It clearly identifies Help Children Thrive as the established nonprofit partner, defines the scope of need (500 children) and speaks to the outcomes – children making happy memories instead of experiencing the discomfort of hunger – rather than outputs...the number of meals served. Bonus points for triggering empathy by inviting the donor to recall their own carefree days of summer as children and for showing donors who they will be helping children in their own community. The full project cost is clear, as is the specific ask being made of the donor. You'll notice the absence of jargon. There are no references to "at risk" youth from households below 125 percent of the poverty line, etc. Finally, this version of the case statement clearly states what's standing in the way of the transformation we're proposing...money!

A full-length version of this case statement could include a few more details. However, this short example is meant to demonstrate how few words are needed to create a compelling case statement. As you think about writing your organization's case for support, how will you answer these questions?

- Who are we?
- Why do we exist?
- What is unique about our organization?

- What do we want to accomplish?
- How do we intend to accomplish it?
- How will we hold ourselves accountable?
- What would happen if our organization went away?

In this chapter, you've learned the case for support is the most important document you can create in fundraising because it creates a compelling and consistent message for all your stakeholders. You know what details to include, and how to use emotional language to speak to the transformations you will create. You've also learned the importance of creating a sense of urgency based on the consequences of not addressing the problem rather than internal, organizational goals that aren't particularly compelling to a prospective donor.

Donors want to be part of the solution and are particularly interested in projects that benefit their local communities. They respond when they see the relevance to their own circumstances, and they need you to paint a picture of what the future could look like. They also want to know how their gifts will make a difference and how you will measure success. In the next chapter, we'll explore strategies for soliciting donors in ways that feel personal to them. These skills are a vital part of developing sustainable funding for your organization.

CHAPTER EIGHT

Making the Ask

In the last chapter, we learned the case for support is the document that outlines the work you are trying to accomplish so every stakeholder can be consistent in their messaging. You began working on the case for support for your organization so by now you should have a program or project you can "sell" to supporters. You will want to frame that project as an opportunity for the donor to create impact by working with you.

In this chapter, we'll explore how to solicit donors in ways that feel very personal to them by speaking to their interests. We will also discuss strategies for using a multi-channel approach for communications in order to increase our chances of closing the deal.

Before we dive in, I'd like you to think about some of the solicitations you receive and how they make you feel. Do you feel more connected to organizations that begin their letters with, "Dear Friend" or those that greet you more personally using your name?

Most donors prefer to be greeted by name and they

expect you to spell their names correctly even if it's a name like "Ramjattan" which is easily misspelled. Donors want to feel like you know them personally, care about their interests and passions, and value their contributions sufficiently so invest your time in getting things right.

Segmentation

Segmentation is the process of categorizing donors based on similar characteristics such as demographics and interests. Smart fundraisers segment donors so they can send out targeted communications that may appeal to donors' interests and ask for the right contribution amount based on past giving history. Segmentation allows you to help your donors understand you know them and value them personally. It makes it easier to build mutually rewarding relationships.

There are many ways to segment your donor lists. There's no right or wrong way to do it. Each nonprofit organization needs to choose a method that fits within their overall strategy for building relationships with donors. Here are a few ways you can segment your audience.

First-time Donors Versus Existing Donors

You may want to create a segment of first-time donors so you can provide additional support and outreach, thereby increasing the likelihood you will retain them. First-time donors have different needs from your existing donors. They don't necessarily know a lot about you, nor do you know a lot about them. As new donors, they may be interested in learning more about volunteering, opportunities to visit your programs, or even how to become monthly donors. Existing donors, on the other hand, already know about you. They are more interested in learning how you used their gifts to create impact.

You can retain significantly more of your first-time donors if you invest additional resources in building relationships with them. One organization that does this really well is Brittany's Hope, a nonprofit that helps abandoned children all over the world. I learned about them when another consultant commented on the fantastic experience she'd had when she made her first gift. Within an hour, the executive director had reached out to her by phone to welcome her to the "family" and ask if she had any questions about how her gift would be used. This is where donor segmentation can help you. If you create a segment for first-time donors, you can customize your outreach to them, increase the frequency of communications in the early weeks of your relationships when you're getting to know each other, and make them feel good about investing in your mission.

Gift Size

Another way to segment donors is by the size of their gifts. By knowing how much your donors give you can determine how much you should ask for during your next campaign. You wouldn't want to ask a donor that had given you $5,000 in a past campaign for a contribution of $100. Nor would you want to request $500 from a donor that had given you $10 previously. When you group donors based on their gift size you can create different versions of an appeal letter or email based on their giving history.

One strategy for renewing gifts is to vary the stories of impact to fit the size of the gift you're asking for. When soliciting a $5,000 gift, for example, you want to tell a story about a project that costs way more than you would for a $25 donor and vice versa. You don't want a major donor to think you're relying on them to provide all the funding for a project. Nor do you want a small donor to think their gift won't have an impact because it's such a small percentage of the total needed to implement the project.

Another gift-size strategy you can use is to score automatic upgrades by increasing suggested gift amounts, so they are slightly above the size of the donor's last gift. If a donor gave $25 last time, your suggested contribution amounts may be $35, $50, $75 or $100 in a subsequent solicitation letter. Even if the donor contributes at the lowest level, they'll still be upgrading their level of support.

Interests

Donors give for a variety of reasons and you want to appeal to those interests to increase the chances of renewing their support. If your organization runs several programs, donors may be interested in a particular program rather than your organization as a whole. You're more likely to renew their financial support if you solicit them with stories based on the program they like, than if you tell a story about another unrelated program that may not be of interest to them.

Acquisition Channel

It is important to understand how your donors were acquired because it can tell you a lot about their preferences and their level of interest. A donor who mails a check, for example, is more likely to prefer being solicited by direct mail. Donors who give online, are more likely to appreciate updates that come via email rather than phone calls or direct mail. Donors who come to your organization via peer-to-peer campaigns contributed because a friend or loved one asked, not necessarily because they know a lot about your organization. If you want to your retain peer-to-peer donors, you'll want to treat them like the first-time donors they are and also remind them how they became connected to your cause.

Giving Frequency

Some donors will give sporadically while others will give each month. Knowing the frequency of your donor's gifts allows you to send the right messages at the right times. You wouldn't speak to a monthly donor, for example, the same way you'd appeal to a lapsed donor who hasn't given in several years. Giving frequency can also help you identify prospects who are highly likely to upgrade their giving. A monthly donor, for example, has the recency, frequency, and affinity to make a larger investment such as a major gift or even a planned gift. On the other hand, a donor who contributed a single gift last year but not this year, will need to be encouraged to reinvest.

Age and Demographics

Each generation is moved by different fundraising techniques. Baby boomers tend to respond better to direct mail than millennials and have more disposable income because they've already raised their families. However, millennials and Generation Z are more likely to setup peer-to-peer fundraising pages and solicit their networks to support your cause. They have less disposable income, are paying off student loans, and raising young families with high childcare costs. While they may not have much to give personally, they are willing to use their influence to fundraise. Older donors also tend to be better prospects for planned gifts as they've already raised their families and are thinking about the legacies they want to leave behind.

Communication Preferences

One of the most important things you need to know about your donors is how and with what frequency they'd like you to communicate with them. The quickest way to alienate a donor is to violate their personal space with unwanted emails or texts. Donors appreciate you asking questions about their preferred channels for communication and the types of stories they'd like to receive because it shows them you value their time; not just their money.

Multi-channel Communications

Now that you've segmented your donors, you'll need to choose the channels you'll need to communicate with them. While donors may have a strong preference for a particular channel (like direct mail or email), this doesn't mean this is the only channel you should use to connect with them.

Donors are just like me and you. They are consumed with the tasks of balancing demanding jobs, busy families, and many other interests. You can't rely on a single email or letter to score a donation. Instead, you need to reach out to donors on multiple channels on multiple occasions. Like paid advertising, the more times they see or hear your message, the more likely they are to take the action you want them to take – give money. This doesn't mean we need to hound them repeatedly until they give. Rather, it is a coordinated approach that uses multiple forms of communication – social media, telephone, email, and direct mail to invite donors to invest.

Studies show that donors who are approached on two or more channels (email, direct mail, or telephone, etc.) contribute more than double the amount than those who are approached using a single channel. Nonprofits that use more than one channel to engage donors also retain a much higher percentage of donors than those that rely on a single channel.

Leveraging Technology

To communicate and engage your donors, it is vital that you have the technology and infrastructure to segment your donors and personalize your communications. You need systems to keep track of your donors' preferences. If a donor tells you they do not want to receive telephone calls or emails, you must be able to honor their preferences or you risk losing them. The only way to track that is with a donor database. Similarly, email marketing software allows you to clone email blasts so you can make minor changes to make communications more relevant to each segment.

The Power of "Old School" Communications

Of course, in a time when technology rules, it's important to remember that "old school" communications are often the most treasured. Donors *love* to receive handwritten thank you notes and cards. These forms of communications feel highly personal and donors appreciate the time and thought you put into writing them.

In this chapter, you've learned the importance of personalizing your communications with donors, so they feel like the valuable partners they are. You've learned that segmentation is the process that makes personalization possible. By dividing donors into groups based on shared characteristics you can create communications that feel very personal to them, but still communicate in large groups for the sake of efficiency. There just aren't enough hours in each day to treat every donor as if they are your only donor, but you can make them feel like you know who they are personally and that you appreciate them. You also learned the importance of communicating with donors in multiple channels because the more often they hear a message, the more likely they are to act on it. In the next chapter, we'll explore simple techniques you can use to delight donors. Happy donors keep giving, so these are important skills for you to develop.

CHAPTER NINE

Delighting Your Donors

Now that you understand how to create a compelling case for support and how to segment your donors so you can speak to them in ways that feel very personal, it's time to turn your attention to the most important job you have as a fundraiser... delighting your donors. You really are in the donor happiness business because happy donors keep giving! The question is, how can you create a culture of donor love?

Loving Your Donors

When I reflect on all the organizations I've ever worked with, the one that had the strongest donor love culture was the Missionaries of the Poor. Their community consisted of highly empathetic and passionate human beings. We were all ordinary people provided with extraordinary opportunities to partner in a mission that resonated deeply within us. And, we had *fun* together. The camaraderie and kinship we felt as volunteers and donors was life-giving. How did they do it?

Whenever someone visited one of their homes for the severely disabled and elderly, the brothers made them feel welcome. Every religious brother, from the senior leadership to those who had just joined the order, went out of his way to thank visitors for coming, answer questions, and make sure they were having a good time. No one could leave one of their homes or special events without having to answer the question, "When are you coming back to see us again?" The brothers understood that the key to growing support for their mission was to treat volunteers and donors as special friends. They went out of their way to shower every guest with love and people came to love them. They had a knack for attracting big-hearted people, many of whom developed life-long friendships. They created an environment where people had *fun* connecting and serving alongside others in the most miserable of circumstances. Joy is contagious!

Volunteers saw firsthand the impact they were making in the lives of people who were homeless, poor, elderly, and disabled. They witnessed the brothers rescuing very sick or abandoned people from the streets and saw the pure joy on the faces of those rescued when they were welcomed into a safe, loving home. Volunteers learned their stories, felt their suffering, and grew frustrated by the unfairness of life. They witnessed joyful brothers working tirelessly to create a happy environment that felt like home, singing while they did chores, joking with residents, and finding ways to make fun adventures out of the monotonous tasks of daily living.

Without the luxury of earned income from government contracts or public safety nets, Missionaries of the Poor relied on the generosity of individual donors. Every person they connected with felt called to help as much as they could, because they knew the needs and impact of this vibrant community, which were communicated several times each year through newsletters with powerful stories.

Ultimately, they were successful in delighting their donors because they helped every volunteer and donor fall in love with their mission, empowered us to get involved, and took the time to build relationships. They got to know their donors, volunteers, and their families. They celebrated with us during times of joy and mourned with us during times of sorrow. They always inquired, "How can we pray for you?" They were and are servant leaders!

Delighting Your Donors is Not Rocket Science

It's not difficult to delight your donors when you make them feel like heroes in every encounter with you. Donors needs are pretty simple. They want you to:

- Promptly and personally thank them when they contribute
- Tell them how you used their gift
- Share heart-warming stories to show the impact their gifts have made
- Ask them for advice

Loyal donors are the result of taking time to care about your supporters, appreciating them, and inviting them into deeper relationships with you. It is also the result of an organizational infrastructure that supports fundraising and development.

The journey you create for donors will inspire them to deepen their relationships with you and increase their commitments. You can never overestimate the importance of remembering this: the longer a donor stays with an organization, the more valuable they become because their retention represents a commitment to your mission and work. Retained donors are treasured partners.

It is cheaper (and less work) to keep the donors you already have than it is to go out and find new ones. Yet many nonprofits make the mistake of prioritizing donor acquisition (finding new donors) over donor retention (renewing existing donors). This is not to say donor acquisition is unimportant. It is a key element of fundraising. However, if you want to increase your individual giving revenue each year and improve your financial sustainability, you'll need to invest more in donor happiness strategies to keep your current donors than you do in finding new ones. Here are a few activities you can implement to make your donors feel like treasured partners:

- Communicate frequently with stakeholders, not just when you need funds
- Treat them as treasured insiders
- Create opportunities for donors to visit and work alongside you so you can get to know them, and they can get to know you
- Pay attention to what's happening in their lives and offer words of encouragement, congratulations, and comfort when needed
- Help them fall in love with your mission and inspire them to become ambassadors for your cause

- Create opportunities for them to lead
- Invest in fundraising technology: a donor database, email marketing tools, your website, and social media channels
- Have clear, concise mission, vision, and case for support statements
- Every stakeholder should be able to articulate these with ease
- Include fundraising and development goals in the job descriptions of every employee
- Include fundraising and development in the agendas of staff and board meetings
- Provide training in "friendraising" so every stakeholder understands how to attract new supporters and retain those already on board

Donors Have Love Languages

It is worth noting that donors and supporters are people, and people give and receive love in different ways. One of my favorite books is, *The Five Love Languages* by psychologist Gary Smalley because it provides valuable insight into the way people express and feel love. If you haven't read this book, the basic premise is there are five love languages:

- Words of Affirmation
- Acts of Service
- Quality Time
- Touch
- Gift Giving

While most people are able to give and receive love in each of these ways, we all have preferred languages and tend to express love in our preferred language. However, the receiver may not feel loved if that is not their preferred language. If your preferred language is gift giving, for example, you will often shower someone with gifts to express your love. However, if their preferred love language is words of affirmation, all the gifts in the world won't mean as much to them as complimenting and affirming them. Similarly, if your preferred love language is quality time, and someone expresses their love for you by praising you rather than giving you their undivided attention, you may never feel the depth of the love they are trying to express.

You can apply these same principles to your supporters. There will be some who prefer to receive recognition and praise for their support while others will prefer to spend quality time visiting with the people you serve and see their impact firsthand. Some will want to make in-kind or financial contributions while others will prefer volunteering their time. This is why it's important to provide a wide array of choices for people to share in your work and get to know your donors so you can express your gratitude for their generosity in ways that are meaningful to them.

When you shower your donors with love, the funds will follow. You'll be able to attract mission-minded people seeking partnerships so they can make a difference. This may seem counter-cultural when you already have more on your plate than you can reasonably handle. Yet it's the most effective way to help your organization grow and develop diversified and sustainable revenue for your mission.

- Think of your own journey as a donor. Do you have a favorite nonprofit?
- Why are they your favorite?
- How do they make you feel?
- What strategies do they use to make you feel like you're special to them?
- How do they recognize your contributions?
- Do they ever ask your opinion or advice?

Why Donor Retention Matters

Dr. Adrian Sargeant, Professor of Philanthropy at the Lily Family School of Philanthropy at Indiana University, is one of the world's most respected voices and researchers in the fundraising field. Through his extensive research and data analysis, he estimates that by increasing donor retention by 10 percentage points a nonprofit can double the amount a database of donors contributes over the life of their partnership with a nonprofit. To put this into perspective, let's say you have a donor file of 1,000 donors who contribute $150,000 and you have a retention rate of 40 percent. If you improve your retention rate by just 10 percentage points to 50 percent, the value of the gifts those donors will make will be around $300,000!

Why Donors Stop Giving

One of the best ways to keep your donors is to figure out what makes them stop giving so you don't alienate them. Dr. Sargeant's research revealed some of the reasons donors leave:

- 5 percent thought the charity did not need them
- 8 percent received no information on how their contributions were used
- 9 percent had no memory of supporting an organization
- 13 percent were never thanked for donating
- 18 percent experienced poor service or communication

The bad news is 53 percent of donors stop giving because of poor communication from the nonprofit they supported. The good news is this situation is entirely fixable by improving donor communications and data hygiene.

The Way You Make Me Feel

Dr. Maya Angelou is famous for saying, "People will forget what you said, people will forget what you did, but people will never forget how you made them feel." This is especially true for your donors. Do your communications make them feel like treasured partners and insiders or ATM machines waiting for the next withdrawal request?

If your organization is like most nonprofits, only four out of every ten of your donors make additional gifts because they feel more like ATM machines than treasured partners. In other words, six out of every ten donors walk away because you don't make them feel like the heroes they are. The question is, how can you fix this? The secret is to spend your fundraising resources wisely. You have limited time. Instead of stretching yourself thin by trying to meet all donors' needs, prioritize the needs of your largest contributors. You *can* delight donors even amidst the never-ending to-do list of every Chief Everything Officer, especially if you are strategic in where you invest your time.

The 80/20 Rule

The 80/20 rule, also known as the Pareto Principle, was developed by Italian economist, Vilfredo Pareto in the late 1800s. Pareto discovered that 80 percent of all economic results were generated by 20 percent of the activities used to generate them. The same is true of fundraising. About 80 percent of our fundraising revenue is generated by 20 percent of our activities. If we apply this to individual giving, 80 percent of the dollars contributed by individuals are donated by the top 20 percent of your donors. Understanding the 80/20 rule can help you learn how to prioritize your tasks, days, weeks, and months especially if you're a Chief Everything Officer with too much to do and very little time. Your goal is to spend most of your energy and resources on the people and activities that generate the most revenue for your bottom line.

Since 80 percent of the donations you receive come from 20 percent of your donors and you have limited time for donor outreach, you'll want to create a VIP list (top 20 percent of donors based on the revenue they contribute). If you have a donor management system or constituent relationship management (CRM) software, this is easy to do. Your software likely includes reports to help you extract this information. If you're keeping track of donations in spreadsheets, this can be a bit more challenging. You may need to seek the help of a fundraising consultant to help.

I recommend also including recurring donors in your VIP list, even if they do not meet the VIP threshold based on the dollars they contribute. Recurring donors are loyal and hugely invested in your cause. Month after month they make your work possible by contributing small gifts that add up over time. Treat them like the VIPs they are so they keep giving.

- Do you know who your top donors are?
- How much time do you spend each week welcoming new donors, thanking donors in a personal way, and visiting major gift donors or prospects?
- What activities consume most of your time?
- Do you spend time getting to know your donors?

Overcoming a VIP Disaster

When Jocelyn, an executive director leading a large social services organization, identified her VIPs, she discovered a major donor had made a six-figure gift about six months earlier and she never received a thank you letter. Jocelyn was horrified. How is it possible that one of the largest gifts to her organization had never been acknowledged? The answer was simple: employee turnover. Embarrassed, and unsure what to do, she sought my advice.

While Jocelyn's initial reaction was to hide from the donor, I asked her, "What do you have to lose by reaching out?"

Nothing! Together we composed a heartfelt handwritten note acknowledging and apologizing for the organization's failure to thank the donor for her generous gift. Jocelyn invited the donor to join her for a cup of coffee so she could see her gift at work. She included with her card, a small batch of gourmet brownies hoping the delicious treat would take the sting out of feeling neglected. How many nonprofits do you know that openly acknowledge their mistakes and send brownies as a way of making amends? Talk about standing out from a crowd!

Within days, the donor called Jocelyn to thank her for the card, the brownies, and to accept her invitation. She was so delighted to be invited that she brought her entire family along. They interacted with the children whose lives they were changing through their philanthropy. Before leaving, they voiced a concern to Jocelyn. What would happen to the children who had outgrown their coats? Winter was fast approaching, and their families would not be able to afford new ones. Without being asked, they requested a list of coat sizes so they could purchase more than 200 winter coats for the children. This gift would never have been received if Jocelyn hadn't overcome her embarrassment by inviting the donor for coffee.

As the holidays approached, I encouraged Jocelyn to invite this donor and her family to attend the Christmas pageant. "I can't invite them to the Christmas show. They're Jewish!" With a big grin I responded, "Jocelyn, Jesus was a JEW! Teach those kids some Hannukah songs and Kwanza songs too. Turn it into a multi-cultural holiday celebration and invite all your donors." Guess what… the donor and her family came to the show and they loved it.

Jocelyn continued to cultivate these donors and was stunned to receive the most surprising gift a few months later. They had doubled the size of their initial contribution! When Jocelyn called to express her gratitude, the donor explained they make six-figure gifts each year to three different organizations. Jocelyn was the only executive director to take the time to thank them much less invite them to visit. They had increased their contributions to Jocelyn's organization and reduced the gifts they sent to the others.

This is why it's important to create a VIP segment so you can spend your time building relationships with the people who are most committed to your cause and make them feel like the heroes they are. When people who believe in your mission feel appreciated and think that you're using their money wisely, they increase their giving.

Donor Love is Donor Stewardship

Stewardship is the process of building relationships with and delighting your supporters. The heartbeats of stewardship are the communications you send out to your supporters. Stewardship is about respect, accountability, kindness, and bringing joy to people's lives. The same kinds of connections that make you a good friend to others, can help you build relationships with donors.

Now that you've segmented your supporters, you'll want to decide what kinds of interactions and communications you'll deploy to nurture relationships:

- Welcome series emails and phone calls for new donors

- Thank you letters for donors within forty-eight h[ours of] receiving a gift
- E-mail updates with success stories they've made possible
- Annual gratitude reports showing the impact you're making together and the challenges that lie ahead
- Invitations to special events
- Phone calls and handwritten cards to say thank you, or "I thought of you today."
- Advice visits with VIP donors

As a general rule of thumb, you'll want to touch supporters three times between asks so they don't feel like ATM machines. Donors should receive an immediate thank you followed by one or more emails or letters with success stories they've made possible and/or invitations to engage further. You'll customize these communications based on the donor's familiarity with your work. New donors or new event attendees, for example, are not familiar with your organization. You need to drop them into a welcome series before you solicit them.

Welcome Series for New Supporters

Message	Timing
Welcome to the family, who we are	Immediately
Invitation to connect on social media	+ Two days
Invitation to visit your program	+ Five days
Appeal	+ Seven days

- How do you welcome, thank and appreciate your donors?
- Are donors thanked personally within forty-eight hours of making a gift?
- Can you create opportunities for donors to visit and see their gifts at work?
- How often do you share success stories with donors?

If you'd like to learn how other nonprofits practice donor love and stewardship, be a secret shopper. Make small gifts to several organizations and see what happens. Which ones make you feel like a treasured partner? How do they do it? Which ones leave you feeling like an ATM machine? What could they have done differently to make you feel like a hero?

Donor Delight Done Right – Welcoming Donors

A few years ago, I was speaking with my colleague, Pamela Grow, one of America's Top 50 Fundraisers, about how to create powerful donor journeys that increase donor retention. "You've *got* to check out Brittany's Hope," she said. "Their stewardship is unbelievable. I got a phone call from the executive director less than thirty minutes after I made my first gift!"

Curious to see if it was a fluke, I went onto their website and made a small gift. Twenty-three minutes later my phone rang. "Hello, Rachel. My name is Mai-Lynn and I'm the executive director of Brittany's Hope. I'm calling to thank you for your very generous gift, to welcome you to the family, and to answer any questions you may have. Would you like to know how we plan to use your gift?"

I played along as the new donor while taking copious notes of our conversation. I eventually confessed to Mai-Lynn that I am a fundraising consultant and made the gift to see whether my friend's experience was a fluke or not. "May I ask you for a few more minutes of your time to tell me how you're able to welcome donors the way you do?" I asked.

I assumed they had a large staff working for them as it didn't seem possible to have this "high touch" response without one. Imagine my shock when Mai-Lynn said they were a tiny staff of four working on a shoe-string budget. How were they able to find time to welcome new donors? They had the help of technology.

Mai-Lynn used a donor management system that sent her a new donor's name, phone number, gift amount, and date and time of gift every time a new donor record was created. Since she set up her mobile phone to receive work emails, she received timely alerts no matter what time of day a donor made their gift. She made it a policy to acknowledge every first-time gift within thirty minutes. Genius! Brittany's Hope demonstrates the value of investing in technology to help you create a powerful and welcoming donor journey.

Donor Delight Done Right — Advice Visits

One of the most powerful ways to delight donors is to ask their advice. Remember the old adage in fundraising, *"If you want advice, ask for money. If you want money, ask for advice."* I've found it to be true. Donors are smart people. They have more than money to offer and they are eager to share their ideas. Many of them have life experience which can be invaluable to your work. By seeking their advice, you have the opportunity to help them acquire deeper knowledge of the problems you are trying to solve making them more likely to want to be part of the solution and their contributions will follow.

You can gather feedback from donors in several ways: donor surveys, focus groups, and one-on-one meetings. The latter is my personal preference because giving a donor your personal attention makes them feel important and they can express themselves freely without worrying about what other people will think.

Donors are busy people so you may find it helpful to offer a variety of ways to connect, get together for a cup of coffee or a quick phone call. Either way, your interview should last no more than thirty minutes and your meeting should be scheduled based on each donor's preference. Let them know that you're doing some research for your organization and would love to ask them a few questions so you can learn from them.

Discovery Questions

You want your meeting to be a warm and friendly conversation rather than a game of 20 Questions to gather information. Open ended and why questions work best. Pauses in conversation give the donor time to think and they will usually open up if you stay quiet. Some of my favorite questions to ask donors are:

- Tell me about your family.

- What led you to your current profession?
- What are your favorite causes and nonprofits to support? Why?
- How did you hear about <insert organization>?
- What inspired you to make your first gift to <insert organization >?
- What kinds of updates do you like to receive? Why?

Donor Delight Done Right — Reporting Impact

The key to being able to make your donors feel good about the investments they've made in your work is to create a communications calendar. The sample calendar below shows how you can engage supporters by making the most of holiday observances.

Communications for Existing Supporters and Donors

Month	Communication
January	Donor or volunteer thank you and year-end gift summary
February	Donor or volunteer appreciation piece to coincide with Valentine's Day
March	Spring appeal or special event followed by thank you and story

April	Spring is a time for new beginnings success story
May	Mother or Father's Day-themed success story or donor appreciation piece
June	Summer appeal
July	Donor story with impact success story
August	Volunteer story with impact success story
September	Client success story
October	Donor thank-a-thon (board members call donors to say thanks)
November	Year-end appeal kicked off on Giving Tuesday
December	Success stories throughout the month with *donate* call to action for donors who have not yet contributed to the year-end appeal.

You can complete your calendar by creating messaging for each segment you identified earlier. (Since recurring donors are already supporting your work each month, you'll want to replace their appeals with progress reports on the work you are doing together. However, you can solicit them again during the year-end appeal and ask them to consider increasing their monthly gift.)

In this chapter, you've learned that happy donors keep giving and increase the size of their gifts over time. The quickest way to developing sustainable revenue for your organization is to focus your attention on welcoming and bringing joy to the lives of your existing donors and supporters. People are curious. They want to know what happened as a result of their contributions. Donors want to feel good about their decision to invest in your work and have confidence that you'll do great things with their money. You don't have to get everything right. Donors will tolerate a lot when they feel loved and appreciated, so if you don't do anything else, focus on making them happy and express your gratitude to them constantly. Be personal. Be authentic. Be grateful. Delighting your donors is a team sport. In the next chapter, we'll explore how to get your board on board and empower them to help you build strong relationships with donors.

CHAPTER TEN

Getting Your Board on Board

Now you understand how important it is to focus your efforts on keeping your donors happy despite the challenges of making time to do it. The good news is you don't have to do all the work yourself. Your board of directors can help you with donor love and stewardship if you empower them to do it. You may be thinking, *Yeah, right! I can't get my board to do anything*. That may be true, but it doesn't mean you can't turn things around. The first step in getting your board on board, is for you to understand how board members think. Breaking news. No one joins your board because they wanted to fundraise!

Reluctant board members are slow to help you fundraise for a reason. They may not feel confident in their public speaking skills. They may fear rejection, so they feel uncomfortable asking people for money or inviting others to get involved. They may not know what to say when they talk about your organization. Or, they may not realize that there are many ways to support fundraising. It's not always about asking people for money.

Some of your board members may be introverts at heart

and shy away from asking people for money while others that are more extroverted may be quick to volunteer to solicit their networks. Regardless of the reason board members don't participate, you can find ways to engage reluctant board members in fundraising and donor love and equip them to be successful. It is your responsibility to uncover their fears and provide them with the support and resources they need to feel confident.

The key to turning your board members into fundraising superheroes is to recognize that each has different gifts to offer and their personalities and preferences will vary. You have to be creative in developing fundraising and donor love tasks in a way that caters to their strengths while minimizing their fears.

An introverted board member will likely balk at the idea of making an appeal to a large group at a special event. They'd much rather accompany you to a meeting with a major gift prospect – especially if you'll do the heavy lifting of making the ask, while they participate by making the introduction. Introverts may also be open to writing personal thank you notes to donors – especially if you provide them with a few heartfelt examples to follow. A highly social and energetic extrovert, on the other hand, may be a prime candidate for organizing a special event, making a pitch to a large group of supporters, or going out into the community to recruit corporate sponsors.

Which of the following fundraising tasks may be better suited for board members who are introverts? Which ones are extroverted board members more likely to enjoy?

- Sending handwritten thank you notes to donors

- Canvassing the community to find corporate sponsors for an event
- Researching donors' giving interests and capacities
- Making phone calls to donors to thank them for their gifts
- Asking a major gift prospect for a contribution
- Keeping track of ticket sales to a special event
- Soliciting items to sell at a silent auction
- Taking photos of donors having fun at a special event

Turn Board Members into Fundraising Superheroes

Cater to Their Strengths

To be successful, board members need to feel like they are operating in their zone of genius so they can be confident when they engage others. When we pull them out of their comfort zones and ask them to participate in activities, they feel ill-prepared for, they quickly flee. Their strengths are also tied to their passions. Chances are, the things they are good at, are also things they enjoy. The more you give them the opportunity to function in their zone of genius and do things they enjoy, the harder they will work for you.

Give Them Choices

As humans, we are hard-wired to make choices. When we are told what to do and given little choice in the matter, it can get our hackles up. If your board members are anything like me, they will consciously or sub-consciously resist when given only one choice. When you give board members choices in the ways they can contribute, they are much more likely to respond positively to your requests. In their book, *Train Your Board (and Everyone Else) to Raise Money*, fundraising consultants Andy Robinson and Andrea Kihlstedt include a wonderful "all-you-can-eat menu" exercise with a list of fundraising and development activities board members can participate in. After completing the exercise, they'll see there are many ways to assist with fundraising and development and not all of them include making the ask for money.

Make Fundraising Easy by Setting Them Up for Success

If you want board members to raise money successfully, you have to make the process easy and fun. Like you, board members are busy. They are likely working full time, juggling family responsibilities, and making time to volunteer. Already stretched, anything that seems too difficult or time-consuming is likely to be assigned as the eleventh item on their top 10 to-do list. One way to do this is to arm them with collateral materials and emails they can distribute easily. If you want them to invite guests to an event, prepare an enticing email invitation with the link to purchase tickets so all they have to do is copy and paste into a new email and send to their networks. If you need them to help you find corporate sponsors, arm them with sponsorship packets containing the details and a letter or email they can copy and paste to prospective sponsors.

Train Them on Key Fundraising Skills

When board members say they don't like to fundraise, it's probably because they've never been trained how to do it. Yet all of them know how to build relationships with people. The key is to help them recognize their transferable relationship building skills in the context of fundraising. The best way to do that is to include a skill-building exercise as part of every board meeting. Two of my favorite resources are *Train Your Board (And Everyone Else) To Raise Money* by Andrea Kihlstedt and Andy Robinson, and *Friendraising: Community Engagement Strategies for Boards Who Hate Fundraising but Love Making Friends* by Hildy Gottlieb. Both of these books contain simple board fundraising training exercises designed to take no more than fifteen to twenty minutes each.

Arm Them with Inspiring Success Stories

In the 1980s two of the most popular TV shows were Dynasty and Falcon Crest. Monday morning conversations around the water cooler often included talk about the latest plot twists. You need to provide your board members with powerful stories of client transformations that are so compelling they want to share them with their friends. You can share stories in board reports but experiencing "the feels" helps them to remember the stories and get excited about the impact your organization is creating. Invite a client to each board meeting to give a testimonial so board members come to understand the nature and scope of your impact.

Help Them Tap into Their "Why"

Every person who joins your board has a "why." Some may be seeking ways to build their resume. Others may be looking for a way to acquire new skills. Perhaps they may have been personally affected by the social impact or cause your organization is working to address. They have specific reasons for taking leadership positions by joining the board. When you understand their "why," you will gain valuable insight into the types of activities that will be most appealing to them. When I was working for Catholic Charities in Miami, one of our board members was assigned to St. Luke's Addiction Recovery Center to help fundraise. As the rector of the local seminary, he was looking for ways to engage his students – future pastors – because he knew they would encounter people struggling with addictions in their future ministries. He worked alongside me to launch and champion an annual Recovery Walk and many of his seminarians were successful at fundraising because they had been personally affected by addiction in their families. Understanding this board member's "why" helped me to create an event that not only raised money but helped him meet the needs of his students.

Praise and Recognition

Like most humans, board members feel good when their good deeds are recognized and appreciated. This is particularly true when board members are asked to fundraise. They can become very competitive. Every board meeting should include a report showing the progress each board member is making towards their fundraising goals. Peer pressure is a wonderful thing. When board members see their peers outshining them, they will often step up their game.

Ride along until They Feel Confident

While board members may be fearful of fundraising, you can often get them to join in if you "ride along" with them as they try new things. If a board member is making calls to donors, they may be more comfortable if they can watch you make a call first, practice making a call with you, then have you alongside them as they call their first donor. Once they see that they have all the skills needed to be successful, they'll be ready to go it alone. It's a bit like teaching a child to ride a bike. In the beginning, you run beside them even though they have training wheels. As they grow more confident, you stop running alongside them and let the training wheels support them. Before you know it, the training wheels are off, and they are riding like the wind. The same is true of your board members. You'll get them to work harder in fundraising if you walk alongside them until they have the confidence to do it alone.

Help Them Identify Their Circles of Influence

No doubt you've come across board members who will tell you they can't fundraise because they don't know any rich people. Most people who join your board have never sat down to take an inventory of the people they know. This is particularly true of introverts. One of my favorite exercises is from Hildy Gottlieb's book, *Friendraising: Community Engagement Strategies for Boards Who Hate Fundraising but Love Making Friends.* The "Who Do You Know" exercise asks board members to write down the names of the people they know and prompts them to think about who they know. Who is your hairdresser, banker, tax accountant, or insurance broker, etc. After twenty minutes of writing names down, board members will see that they have a bigger circle of influence than they thought. The average board member will know 100-120 people on that list. Once they know who they know, you can help them figure out the best way to introduce those folks to your organization.

Get Their Hands Dirty

Board members need to work with their heads, feel with their hearts, and experience with their hands if you want them to become good fundraisers. Schedule board members for "a day in the life" event where they spend a day with your program staff interacting with clients. This gives them the opportunity to meet the people being helped face to face, to ask questions, and feel empathy for the hardships they experience. Instead of telling a story about John Doe, now they are in a position to tell a story of John, someone they've met face to face. Day in the life events also help them to understand the work your organization does to solve complex problems because they will have seen you and your staff take action.

In this chapter, you've learned that even the most unenthusiastic board can be empowered to get involved in fundraising if you provide them with the right support. You need your board to work alongside you if you're going to develop sustainable revenue for your organization. Fundraising success requires you to train more people to ask. You cannot rely on yourself alone. The more people working together, the more money you'll raise. In the next chapter, you'll learn how to create an infrastructure and culture with built-in accountability measures that make fundraising a central priority for your entire organization.

CHAPTER ELEVEN

Make Fundraising a Central Leadership Priority

In the last chapter, you learned how to empower board members to become fundraising champions for your organization. In this chapter, you'll turn your attention to creating policies and procedures for your organization to establish fundraising expectations for every role and nurture accountability. Fundraising is a team sport. Every person who works for or volunteers with your organization can play a role. However, you need to have policies and procedures in place that convey this responsibility to all your stakeholders.

Fundraising in Job Descriptions

Every board, volunteer, and staff job description in your organization should include some task related to fundraising if you want to make fundraising a central leadership priority for your organization. Job descriptions set the tone for what is expected of each stakeholder. Why not include fundraising?

Board Members

You can include fundraising and development activities in board member job descriptions by assigning them tasks like:

- Making a gift and inviting others to join them in giving
- Introducing you to potential donors
- Participating in discovery conversations with prospective donors to figure out what kinds of projects they like to support
- Hosting intimate donor cultivation events in their homes to find new donors
- Writing thank you letters
- Visiting or calling donors to express gratitude for their support
- Selling tickets and sponsorships to your events

Volunteers

You can also include fundraising and development activities in volunteers' job descriptions. They are your organization's eyes and ears in the community — and the community's eyes and ears to perceive your organization. There are many tasks well-suited to volunteers like:

- Entering donations in your donor management system
- Researching grant opportunities that are a good fit for your organization
- Helping to organize and host fundraising or donor appreciation events
- Writing thank you letters to donors

- Assisting with the preparation of direct mail campaigns
- Recruiting fundraisers for peer-to-peer fundraising campaigns
- Selling tickets to and sponsorships for special events
- Assisting with planning, designing materials, and preparing for fundraising events

Employees

Every employee, from the receptionist to social workers and program directors can be responsible for fundraising. Your receptionist is your *Director of First Impressions* and is the first staff member supporters will encounter when they visit your site. He or she is the best person to gather valuable information like names and email addresses through a simple sign-in sheet and they are perfectly positioned to distribute welcome packets or flyers for upcoming events.

Social workers and program directors ought to be responsible for submitting a certain number of success stories each month. They can also be assigned responsibility for organizing and hosting a special event or raising a certain amount of revenue from grants, corporate sponsors, or individuals.

All employees can take responsibility for sending thank you cards or hosting donor appreciation events. Of course, your employees will need the help of the lead fundraiser to execute these plans successfully. However, writing fundraising and development activities into the job descriptions of your staff sets the expectation that fundraising is a central leadership priority for every staff member.

Paving the Way for Success

Like your board members and volunteers, employees will join your organization with varying amounts of skill and confidence in fundraising. They will need the same support from you as board members do if they are to be successful. One way to accomplish this is to talk about fundraising during the welcome or onboarding process. Every orientation should include information not only about the expectation that all employees and volunteers will participate in fundraising, but also the reassurance that they won't have to do it alone. You'll be responsible for giving them the tools and training to be successful. The most important thing you do during the orientation process is getting their buy-in. You have to explain why fundraising is a team sport at your organization. The bottom line is that even though they volunteer their time, or work for wages that are well below the market rate of for-profit companies, these sacrifices don't equip you to keep the lights on. There are some things only money can do!

Board Governance: Give or Get Policy

If you've ever applied for a grant from a foundation before, no doubt you'll have run into the question, "What percentage of your board contributes financially to your organization?" Foundations ask this question because if 100 percent of your board members who know the good, the bad, and the ugly of your organization, are willing to invest their hard-earned dollars in your organization, then they figure it's safe for them to do so, too. When competition for grant funding is high, the decision on whether you get funded or not can often come down to this question. Funders prefer to fund organizations whose board members provide financial support than those that don't. That's why they ask the question.

One of the most difficult challenges executive directors face is getting board members to make a financial gift. You have to overcome the objection that board members raise… "I already give you my time." And it is true. They do. However, time doesn't keep the lights on, nor does it satisfy funders that believe if board members don't trust you with their money, they shouldn't either.

One way to overcome this challenge is to ensure your board has a Give or Get policy which states every board member will make a financial commitment to the organization. There are two ways to specify the commitment. The first is a specific minimum, for example, each board member will contribute or raise $1,000 for your organization each year. I'm not a fan of this approach as you run the risk of excluding people who cannot afford to contribute or raise funds to that level. I much prefer stipulating that each board member will make a "personally significant gift" defined as, "XYZ organization will be in the top three nonprofits you support financially each year by total dollars contributed." This is a far more inclusive approach. Regardless of the method you use to define the expectation for financial contributions, you do need to get board members to commit each year. Once they commit, you need to report on their progress individually throughout the year, so they don't find themselves at the end of the year having to come up with a large sum they don't have. In the spirit of making things easy, I encourage my board members to divide their contribution into twelve monthly gifts and set up a recurring gift via credit card to make it easy for them to fulfill their obligation.

There are many variations to the Give or Get policy. Some organizations prefer to call it a Count Me In policy – what can we count on you to do to sustain this organization? You can include expectations which are non-financial too, like meeting attendance, serving on committees, and recruiting volunteers, etc. Regardless of the format you choose, a Give *and* Get or a Give *or* Get policy is the best way to ensure your board members contribute financially.

Recruitment and Orientation

One reason so many organizations have "do nothing" boards is because they fail to outline the commitments future board members make if they choose to accept a role on your board. If during the recruitment process you are open with candidates that every board member is expected to make a personally significant gift and help your organization acquire new donors, there won't be any surprises. Board members join your board knowing they'll have to fundraise and with your support, are highly likely to do it. When board members are not aware of these expectations before they agree to serve, that's when resistance happens. You hear, "I didn't sign up for this."

Similarly, during the recruitment and orientation process for volunteers, you need to talk about how your organization is funded. It's important for volunteers to understand where the money comes from to do good work and set the stage for asking them to not only volunteer but to donate, too. Your welcome and orientation process should feature the opportunity to become monthly donors and explain that small gifts of any amount, when given monthly, add up to big impact over time. Volunteers are 70 percent more likely to donate to an organization they donate their time to, because they know where the money is going and can see the impact of their investment firsthand. Organizations that fail to solicit volunteers up front are leaving money on the table. Your volunteers support other nonprofit organizations financially, why not yours?

Rewarding Success

Positive reinforcement is a powerful motivator so it's important to recognize and reward the hard work and fundraising successes of all your stakeholders. The more you recognize their efforts, the harder they will work for you. If you're having a fundraising event, ask your guests to show their appreciation for the hard work of your volunteers through a round of applause. Mention them in printed materials. Host appreciation luncheons for them. Give service awards – lots of them – to volunteers, board members, and your staff.

In this chapter, you've learned how to make fundraising a central leadership priority for your nonprofit by including fundraising activities in the job descriptions of every stakeholder and in board governance documents. You've also learned how to set expectations for fundraising contributions when you recruit and welcome board members, volunteers, and staff. You know that setting the stage is only the first task. You have to support people, so they grow more confident and become the fundraising champions you need. In the next chapter, we'll take a look at some of the obstacles you will face when you try to raise more money for your nonprofit and how to overcome them.

CHAPTER TWELVE

Obstacles and Opportunities

In the last chapter, you learned how to make fundraising a central leadership priority for your organization and a team sport. Here's the thing…fundraising is hard work. You're going to run into obstacles along the way. How you respond to them will determine whether you succeed or fail. You have to let go of the limiting beliefs that you face stiff competition from other nonprofits and a scarcity of dollars and donors. It simply is not true. Yes, there are lots of nonprofits doing great work, but how many of them are good at showering their donors with love and making them feel like heroes? We've already established that there is plenty of money available to nonprofits. You just need to know where to go to find it.

One of my favorite athletes of all time is former Chicago Bulls basketball star, Michael Jordan. That man could pull a win out of nowhere! I remember watching him come from behind to win a basketball game while he was sick with pneumonia. His "can do" attitude and refusal to accept defeat made him the champion he is. His philosophy was simple.

"Obstacles don't have to stop you. If you run into a wall, don't turn around and give up. Figure out how to climb it, go through it, or walk around it."
Michael Jordan

You're probably thinking, "That's cool but I'm no Michael Jordan!" Here's what I know. Every single person who wants to change the world, is going to run into obstacles – including me!

I honed my fundraising skills with the Missionaries of the Poor, a large volunteer-based organization of highly empathetic and passionate human beings. We were ordinary people provided with extraordinary opportunities to partner in a mission that resonated deeply within us. We had *fun* together. The camaraderie and kinship we felt as volunteers was life-giving. You can imagine my excitement when I was hired for my first professional fundraising role in the United States. I couldn't wait to get started! If we could be so effective in a developing country, how much more effective could I be working with skilled professionals in a more affluent country? I assumed every nonprofit in the United States had energetic, passionate volunteers like me eager to help and plenty of donors with the capacity to give. Within days, it became apparent that my new adventure would be a very different assignment. I encountered one obstacle after another and so will you.

Resistance from Program Staff

One of my first tasks was contacting each of the program directors to introduce myself, listen to their fundraising needs, and work with them to develop a plan to achieve their fundraising goals. All they had to do was arm me with stories to share with donors so we could implement a year-round communications plan with multiple solicitations. While the initial meetings were positive, there was no follow-through. One deadline after another passed. No one submitted stories and after a while, they stopped answering emails and phone calls. I became highly frustrated. I decided to get out of my office and visit each program to gather the stories myself. What an eye-opening experience!

Many staff did not see fundraising as their responsibility. They were already stretched thin, without the resources they needed to be effective. Already working long hours, staff were burned out and frustrated. Story gathering was their absolute lowest priority when they had long queues of clients waiting to be served, and not enough staff or resources to help. Rather than express frustration at their failure to do their part, I requested permission to observe their case management sessions and chat with clients afterwards. In one day, I could gather enough photos, stories, and signed media release forms to tell their stories without adding to the workload of staff.

The staff began to see me as an ally, instead of viewing me as one more person from headquarters adding to their already overflowing workloads and complaining when they didn't follow through. They learned I was not afraid to roll up my sleeves to help. We had productive conversations about how we could tweak intake forms, case management notes, discharge forms, and our website, to make the story gathering process easier. As we raised funds together, they began to see the WIIFM (What's in It for Me?) of our partnership. The key to earning buy-in from staff was to become an advocate and ally, rather than another customer they needed to serve. Win-win partnerships empowered program directors to accomplish their fundraising goals with a little help from me. And guess what...we had *fun* together!

How do your program staff feel about fundraising? How can you better support them, so they see you as an ally? What barriers do you need to overcome together to fundraise successfully?

Resistance from Your Board of Directors

The second obstacle of my fundraising assignment was what my executive director described as a "do nothing" board of directors. To better understand their relationships to the organization, I began to attend board meetings. I got to know them and build relationships. They were a group of highly accomplished, well-connected individuals. They were busy people, very engaged in the governance and oversight of the organization, and they attended board meetings faithfully. Why did the executive director and program directors have difficulty getting them involved with fundraising?

I soon learned there was no onboarding process to welcome new board members. They were not required to contribute or raise money. Fundraising discussions, progress reports, and training were not part of their board meetings. While board members were invited to events, and even matched with individual programs as sponsors, they had not been empowered or held accountable for fundraising. With no support from staff how could they be expected to raise funds?

I began meeting with board members one-on-one to learn about their affiliations with the programs they were assigned to. Some board members expressed interest while others had no meaningful attachment to the program they sponsored. Further conversations revealed that some board members were willing to fundraise if asked and given the tools. Others had no interest in fundraising at all.

I quickly identified the early adopters and sparked friendly rivalries among them. We introduced *give and get* policies, gift acceptance policies, annual commitment forms, and peer review processes to set right-sized expectations and hold board members accountable. I worked behind the scenes to set them up for success, creating personal fundraising pages for those that didn't feel comfortable creating them on their own, drafting emails and social media posts they could share with their networks, and making sure even the smallest of fundraising accomplishments were celebrated. I even distributed star-shaped lapel pins they could wear proudly for each fundraising goal they achieved. They wore those inexpensive pins proudly like five-star generals! The early adopters provided social proof that fundraising can be *fun* and inspired other board members to become involved.

When boards resist participation in fundraising it's usually because they weren't aware of their obligation to fulfill this role, they haven't been trained on how to do it, or they are fearful of soliciting their networks and being told no. If you want your board to raise money, you have to get their buy-in, support them, and set them up to win. Then, you must provide affirmation at every possible opportunity.

How does your board feel about fundraising? What reports, training, and feedback do you provide for tracking fundraising goals and progress? Do you have the policies in place to hold board members accountable? How do you set board members up for success?

Executive Director Doesn't Want to Take Risks

The third obstacle I had to overcome was an executive director who was hesitant to take risks. How could I grow fundraising revenues if I didn't have the freedom to try new approaches? To find common ground, I tried to put myself in her position. If we lost money, she would ultimately be responsible for the finding the resources to pay the bills. That's a lot of pressure. Yet if we succeeded, there was huge upside for our bottom line.

I devised strategies for winning her buy-in. First, I found ways to generate positive cash flows so she would not have to ante up cash to underwrite fundraising expenses. Strategies like selling sponsorships, early-bird tickets, and advertisements in event programs all generated positive cash flow. Second, I mitigated risks by creating fallback options. When I wanted to test direct mail acquisition campaigns, for example, I found a vendor willing to fund a pilot. Our contract was contingent on the pilot meeting certain benchmarks. Third, I created key performance indicators to assess fundraising effectiveness. This meant she could hold me accountable for the investments we made and generate data to assess what worked and what didn't work. Finally, I set her up for the win. Each month, I armed her with fundraising reports and board progress reports she could present during board meetings. As our fundraising successes grew, so did the board's view of her business acumen and their willingness to help fundraise. My executive director could claim these victories as her own and demonstrate her commitment to putting the organization on the path to sustainable funding for our mission.

Time Management

One of the most challenging aspects of fundraising is juggling competing responsibilities and the inevitable tasks that land on your desk because no one else knows how or wants to do it. While your title may be "executive director" or "development director," you're really the Chief Everything Officer, official fire starter, troubleshooter, and complaint department all rolled into one. You may be feeling a bit like an acrobat keeping dozens of plates spinning at once by running from one to the other, rotating the sticks that hold them up. Fundraising may feel like the eleventh item on your top 10 to-do list, but you need to prioritize it because fundraising is the *only* way to raise money to run your programs. Here are three strategies you can use to ensure important tasks don't get run over by tasks that seem urgent.

Show Me the Money, Honey

Prioritize your tasks based on those that will make an impact on *your* bottom line. If you have competing tasks such as drafting an appeal letter versus sending a report to your finance department, get your appeal letter written first! You're being evaluated on the amount of money you raise, not on the timeliness of your submissions to the finance department.

Block Scheduling

Block off large chunks of time on your calendar for your important tasks so when others are scheduling meetings, they know you are busy. I try to block times that are low frequency meeting times like Friday afternoons and early mornings, so others are less likely to be disrupted. You may want to reserve one hour each day, for example, to send handwritten thank you notes, make phone calls to major gift prospects, and host donors and prospects for site visits. Use block scheduling for the activities you know help retain donors and find new ones.

Technology Can Help You Improve Your Efficiency

Create inbox rules to tame your email by automatically moving messages with content that includes certain words to email folders. Messages which contain the words "buy now," for example, can go directly to trash. Tools like Hootsuite allow you to schedule social media posts in advance, so you don't get distracted and sucked into rabbit holes when you post content on social media. Google Alerts can help you keep track of donors, board members, and other important stakeholders so you can send appropriate congratulations and sympathy messages, etc. Canva.com helps you create professional-quality images in minutes. Pixabay.com offers millions of royalty free images you can use. The Showcase of Fundraising Innovation and Inspiration website: www.Sofii.org offers thousands of creative fundraising ideas and templates. Most states have a State Association of Nonprofit Organizations that offer affordable training and networking opportunities.

Working Smarter, Not Harder

The key to maintaining your "fundraising mojo" is to make sure you don't reinvent the wheel and you seek out opportunities to grow. Before you create a resource from scratch, search for downloadable templates you can use to get started. You'll spend far less time creating resources this way and you may come across ideas you had not thought of. SOFII's annual IWITOT (I Wish I Thought of That) libraries contain countless, creative ideas you can borrow.

Of course, like any profession, investing in yourself is the key to becoming a successful fundraiser. Seek out opportunities to acquire new skills through professional development. If you really want to increase your impact quickly, consider investing in a personal fundraising coach. You'll want to find a seasoned fundraising expert that has spent time working in the trenches with the kind of organizations you serve, getting the kind of results you're hoping to achieve. Your coach should have experience working with nonprofits of a similar size, stage of development and structure. And he or she must be able to help you craft a fundraising plan that takes advantages of new opportunities while working within the constraints you face. Most of all, your fundraising coach should feel like a mentor and trusted friend. You need to be able to talk freely about your challenges and count on this person to help you, *"Figure out how to climb it, go through it, or walk around it."*

If you're interested in leadership training, contact your local community foundation, American Fundraising Professionals chapter, or a capacity building provider like the Center for Nonprofit Excellence. Many community foundations offer capacity building grants to underwrite the costs of hiring consulting expertise, participating in training programs, and purchasing fundraising technology.

The Bottom Line

Fundraising is hard work and you will face many obstacles. However, this is a problem you need to solve if you want to strengthen and expand your programs, create more impact, and ensure the good work you have begun can continue long into the future. It makes me sad that most people aren't willing to tackle the problem of building sustainable revenue for their organizations. Lack of money is a highly solvable problem if you are willing to invest sufficient time and resources, and train others to help you.

In the last twenty-five years, I've helped hundreds of nonprofits raise more than $25 million and trained nonprofit leaders just like you to raise money for their organizations. I have the skills, experience, and resources to help you raise more money quickly and help you become a powerful and influential fundraiser. With me and my team on your side, you won't have to worry about what will work, whether you'll be making a mistake, or where to spend your time for the greatest impact. I will guide you through the process, help you work efficiently so you don't feel overwhelmed, and help you come up with ideas and communications that will delight your donors.

CHAPTER THIRTEEN

Where Do You Go from Here?

Congrats! You've made it through the process of learning how to become a powerful and inspiring fundraiser capable of raising enough money to fully fund your nonprofit's mission. Now you know that to fundraise like a champion you need to:

- Create a fundraising plan
- Rethink your fundraising mindset
- Understand what donors want but won't tell you
- Create a compelling case for support
- Make the ask
- Delight your donors
- Get your board on board
- Make fundraising a central leadership priority

For the last decade, I've literally trained thousands of nonprofit leaders around the country how to raise money for their missions. The most frequent complaint I hear is, "Why is fundraising so *hard*?" It's hard because you need time to build up the fundraising muscles to be successful and teach others to do the same. Most people give up because they feel discouraged and overwhelmed thinking, they have to do it alone.

Here's what I want you to know about getting people to give you money. It isn't about the tactics, though there are many in this book you can apply to your fundraising (and I hope you do!). It's about being personal, being authentic, and changing your mindset. Fundraising is not about how much money you need to run your programs. It's about giving people the opportunity to change the world and making sure they feel good about the impact they've made through your partnership.

Here's the secret. It's easy to quit trying to find new donors and keep the ones you have. It's easier to write a few grants that will bring in large sums of money at one time. However, neither of those options will help you achieve your dream of being able to hire enough staff to run your programs without worrying about how you'll meet payroll next week. You could just stay right where you are. Or, you can step out of your comfort zone and commit yourself to the hard work of raising money from individuals, trusting that the money will come if you care about what you can do for donors more than what they can do for you.

As you go about implementing the steps you've learned in this book, I want you to reward yourself. Pat yourself on the back as you step outside your comfort zone and try new things. Surround yourself with people and resources that can help you succeed. Most of all, celebrate each day that comes as a new opportunity to make new friends that share your passion for your cause.

You have the right strategy. It's up to you to take action on the tactics and implement them despite all the daily fires that are going to come up and need to be extinguished. You will always have fires to put out. However, you can structure your time to prioritize fundraising because it is the only activity you can do that will generate revenue for your programs. When you look at other organizations that are raising money successfully, it's not necessarily true that they have more resources or better boards of directors. What they have is a committed leader like you working to build the fundraising muscles of their board and team so they can go out into the community and be ambassadors for their cause.

Raising money from individuals is the single best way to reach your goal of fully funding your programs and reducing cash flow problems. When you are the best in the world at making donors feel good about investing in your work, you don't have to "beg people for money." You'll attract investors who trust you to deliver world class solutions to solve problems they care about. This is the mindset of abundance. Yes, there are lots of nonprofits out there asking for money but pitifully few are achieving, and reporting outcomes donors feel proud of.

That's what I want for each of you, to have donors contributing, renewing, and upgrading their financial support providing ample dollars for you to change the world. You have the strategy. You have the tactics. Now, go raise some money and make the world a better place.

ACKNOWLEDGMENTS

First, I have to thank my parents who set the trajectory of my life by loving me unconditionally, choosing to raise me in a mixed income neighborhood in Jamaica, and instilling in me the call to serve others. Mom, you may no longer live with us this side of heaven, but you are with me every day, and I know you are proud of me. You taught me to be a servant leader committed to bringing joy to the lives of every person I meet. Dad, you are responsible for so many of the formative experiences that made me fall in love with this profession. Your constant encouragement and absolute certainty that I can do anything gives me wings to fly. I hope this book makes you proud.

Second, I want to thank my children, Tim, Adam, and Katie. I'm so grateful to be your mum. Thank you for supporting my dreams and encouraging me every step of the way. Tim, watching you chase your dreams, inspires me to chase my own. Adam, your wonderful sense of humor and fearless ability to overcome obstacles motivates me to work harder and never take myself too seriously. Katie, my queen of "good enough," you challenge me to remember that perfection is overrated and done beats perfect every time. Thank you all for bringing out the best in me and for your unconditional and never-ending love. I love you!

Thank you to my siblings, Martin, Sarah, Maggie, Tina, and Thomas, my Chief Encouragement Officers and sparring partners. You have been with me through the best of times and the worst of times and always have my back. When I doubted myself, you encouraged me to step out into the deep, take risks and be confident. Thank you for your constant love and for making me an aunt to the two best nephews on the planet, Julien and Lucas. I love you all.

Huge gratitude to my mentors, coaches and friends: Angela Lauria, Faith Clarke, Pamela Grow, Brian Lauterbach, Nate Nasralla, and Kristen Mackey. I have learned so much from you all and I treasure the special friendships we share. Each of you has reminded me that I am capable of far greater things than I give myself credit for. You have encouraged me to dream bigger and chase those dreams. Kristen, each day I hear your challenge to "own my greatness" and shine. Thank you!

My Network for Good family, especially Travis Centers, and Jack Murphy, my partners on the Impact and Sustainability team and friends for life. Never have I worked alongside a team of "do gooders" that I love so much. You are the reason I look forward to waking up every day, eager to see what adventures await. You are definitely among my favorite humans on the planet.

Carol Mastroianni, thank you for inspiring the title of this book! When I asked you what your fundraising dream was and you said, "No more duct-tape fundraising," the image that popped into my head was pure magic.

Ryan Shultz, I'm immensely grateful for your eye-catching book cover and creativity. You have mad talent as a graphic artist and I feel fortunate our paths crossed.

I owe a debt of gratitude to the hundreds of nonprofit leaders who chose me to be their coach and the more than 100 foundations and capacity building partners nationwide that afford me the honor of working alongside their grantees to help nonprofits become more financially sustainable. You inspire me to bounce out of bed each morning eager to take on the world. Thank you all!

Special thanks to The Author Incubator crew: Cheyenne Giesecke, Mehrina Asif, Emily Tuttle, and Ramses Rodriguez. Without your hard work and dedication, this book would never have seen the light of day.

Finally, I'd like to acknowledge the unnamed people who have touched my life in many ways especially those who trusted me to raise money in the early days when I had no clue what I was doing. Experience is the best teacher and I am grateful for the lessons learned along the way and the opportunity to change lives.

ABOUT THE AUTHOR

Rachel Ramjattan is a national fundraiser and master trainer with twenty-five plus years of experience managing nonprofit technology, fundraising, development, and communications for nonprofits of many missions, budgets, and staffing structures. An expert coach, she is accustomed to juggling the many roles of a Chief Everything Officer to raise money, not expenses.

A co-founder of a small nonprofit and the lead fundraiser in a one-person development shop for many years, Rachel understands the challenges of fundraising in small organizations. She has helped hundreds of nonprofits raise more than $25 million by improving donor retention and implementing winning donor stewardship practices powered by right-sized technology.

ABOUT THE AUTHOR

In her role as National Program Director for Impact and Sustainability at Network for Good, Rachel works with more than one hundred funders in the United States to help their grantees develop diversified and sustainable streams of revenue for their missions. When she's not travelling, Rachel lives in Coral Springs, Florida with her family.

Thank You

Thank you so much for reading *The Nonprofit Leader's Guide to Becoming an Inspirational Fundraiser!* If you've made it this far, you're more ready than ever to raise more money to keep your programs running.

I would love to learn more about your fundraising journey and success in funding the work of your organization. Please keep in touch and share your wins with me.

Website: www.nonprofitplusteam.com
LinkedIn: www.linkedin.com/in/rachelramjattan
Facebook: www.facebook.com/nonprofitplusteam
Email: Rachel@nonprofitplusteam.com
Twitter: @RachelNPP

Made in the USA
Coppell, TX
07 May 2021